ON GUARD:
THE FOUR PILLARS OF LEADERSHIP

By

LIEUTENANT COLONEL DANIEL E. HARRIS

With FJ Felsburg

Muddy Boots Leadership, LLC
23B Somerset Dr
P O Box 254
Analomink, PA 18320
www.muddybootsleadership.com

Spoken And Written Words LLC

ON GUARD: THE FOUR PILLARS OF LEADERSHIP

Editor: Christopher G. Murray

Cover Design: John Chomiczewski

Published in the United States by Spoken and Written Words, LLC

ISBN: 978-0-9829976-2-8 (paperback)
978-0-9829976-4-2 (ebook)

Version 1

Printed by Kindle Direct Publishing

Table of Contents

Foreword by Dr. Lamar Blackwell 1
Prologue 3
PART 1 MY JOURNEY 16
Chapter 1 Readiness 17
Chapter 2 Formative Years 22
Chapter 3 Learning About Leadership 28
Chapter 4 My Leadership Trajectory 32
Chapter 5 Deployment and HaDR 37
Chapter 6 Benefits of the Army National Guard 41
PART 2 CLIP 46
Chapter 7 Courage 48
Chapter 8 Love 53
Chapter 9 Integrity 62
Chapter 10 Passion 68
PART 3 OTHER ELEMENTS OF GOOD LEADERSHIP 75
Chapter 11 Listening 77
Chapter 12 Alertness 82
Chapter 13 Don't Just Meet Standards, Exceed Them 86
Chapter 14 Be Decisive 89
Chapter 15 Get Educated 91
Chapter 16 Teamwork and Motivation 95
Chapter 17 Mentorship and Diversity 98
Chapter 18 Millennials vs. Boomers 101
Chapter 19 Multi-domain Leadership 105
PART 4 FIVE LEADERS SHOW THE WAY 111
Chapter 20 Colonel Stephanie Dawson 113
Chapter 21 Colonel Mark Moser 117
Chapter 22 Colonel Carl Pfeiffer 120
Chapter 23 Colonel Dave Cox 126
Chapter 24 General Timothy McKeithen 129
PART 5 CRISIS LEADERSHIP 134
Chapter 25 Katrina and the Waves 136
Chapter 26 True Grit 141
Chapter 27 Lessons Learned from Katrina 145
Chapter 28 The Perfect Storm 148
Chapter 29 Cyber Warfare 155
Epilogue 163
Postscript 167
Acknowledgments 168
Glossary 170

To my granddaughter, Sophia,
and to all of the children of the world
who will grow up to become our future leaders—
and who will serve and be on guard.

Praise for *On Guard*

"In this divisive society (where truth rarely seems to matter and lying is rampant), there's nothing more important than solid leadership. This book tackles the need for Humble Leadership head on. Buy numerous copies and distribute them wisely."
— Patrick B. Ropella, Chairman & CEO of world renowned executive search firm, The Ropella Group, and author of *The Right Hire*

"We were all inspired by great leaders at some point in our lives, whether it was a teacher, a coach or a teammate. On Guard *is a reminder of what leadership once was, and can truly be again."*
— Walter Bond, Hall of Fame Speaker, Former NBA player and author of *Swim! How a Shark, a Suckerfish, and a Parasite Teach You Leadership, Mentoring, and Next Level Success*

"After 30+ years of serving our country, Lieutenant Colonel Daniel E. Harris now serves his readers with insights in his new book on leadership and leaving a legacy."
— Erik Qualman, #1 Bestselling Author of *Socialnomics: How Social Media Transforms the Way We Live and Do Business*

"Leadership simply involves getting people to take action to create an outcome. On Guard offers all leaders an insightful approach to support them in becoming the leader they're intended to be."
— Danny Bader, author of *Back To Life*

"In a world hallmarked by conflict and division, it is downright refreshing to see a leader discuss such quaint notions as love, listening, integrity, and passion. Harris' work will go far in creating the kind of 'human' workplaces many of us are craving."
— Dr. Michael Brenner, Founder & CEO of Right Chord Leadership

"In On Guard: The Four Pillars of Leadership, *Dan Harris weaves a tale both inspiring and educational about selfless service and leadership. Pay close attention to his story, his highly relevant quotes from others, and his illustrative examples of how true leaders reacted to needs and crises. Absorb and apply the lessons, and you'll find the path to success both easier and more enjoyable."*
—Lt. Gen. (Ret.) Gregory Newbold, former Joint Chiefs of Staff Director of Operations

"In my past experience, I have seen three kinds of leaders: 1) Leaders who make things happen; 2) Leaders who watch things happen; and 3) Leaders who wonder what happened. Moreover, you have heard it said time and time again, 'Lead, follow or get out of the way.' If you look closely at leadership, a true leader is a 'servant leader'–a leader who serves those who serve. Lieutenant Colonel Harris is not only a 'servant leader' but a leader who makes things happen for his people and his mission at hand. His book, On Guard: The Four Pillars of Leadership, *delves into those pillars with key examples from his personal perspective about those leaders who make things happen under various stressful circumstances. This book will help you understand the attributes that leaders use to lead and make things happen."*
— Rear Admiral William D. Rodriguez, United States Navy, Retired

"LTC Harris was 'In the Arena.' He knows what it takes to be a great leader in this divided world we find ourselves in today."
—Sharon Wingron, President & Chief PEOPLE Development Partner, DevelopPEOPLE

"If you love stories from the front lines and leadership lessons gleaned from experience, this is your book. Part autobiography of a 30-year ARNG decorated veteran, part how-to leadership guide, and part hero stories, this book covers a lot of ground and is a rich resource about leadership."
—Halelly Azulay, Leadership Development Strategist and Founder at TalentGrow, and host of the *TalentGrow Show* leadership podcast

FOREWORD

What is leadership? Are leaders born or made? If you were to ask me to give you an example of leadership when I was in sixth grade, I would have referred you to doctors, firefighters, and the President of the United States. As I got older, I became more interested in understanding how I might become a leader (actually, my first goal was to get people to listen to me more!). My interest in leadership led me to explore the qualities of a good leader. Here's what I learned.

A good team leader must master the ability to lead *themselves*. They must be able to get from one point and lead themselves to another. When I go to the gym and look for a trainer, the trainer who looks like they have spent some time in that gym would be more credible to me than someone who doesn't look like they're in shape. Why? Without saying a word, they convey the image that they have led themselves into getting into shape. The more experience you have in demonstrating personal leadership, the more you learn about yourself.

One of the things you learn from leading yourself is that most of the fruit is in the journey—not the destination. Good leaders understand that if they respond well during the journey, the destination is a logical conclusion. While other people are more interested in the reward at the end of the journey, leaders know that there will not be a reward at the end without personal development during the process. They understand that the challenges and obstacles along the way are growth opportunities that bring out the best in us. While others are focused on the prize and want to avoid the challenges, good leaders understand that learning how to overcome challenges prepares us for what is next—and ultimately results in the prize at the end.

Good leaders understand that challenges are not just physical, but mental, too. They have learned how to win the battles in their mind. They have learned how to think about a challenge in such a way that it puts them in the right mind and space to execute. Rather than worrying about challenges and avoiding the very thought of them, they expect them. And they plan for them. They are aware of the mental challenges that they had to face. They may not be aware of every possible hurdle, but they know those challenges exist and will need to be addressed if they are to be successful.

Once good leaders are able to successfully lead themselves, they are able to lead others. This is where good leaders really excel. Good leaders understand the journey and have mastered it—but their ultimate mission is helping others achieve success.

Helping others takes more than explaining how to navigate the journey to success. Good leaders get to know their teams on an individual basis. They know that individuals on their team are there for different reasons, which may be very different from their own reasons. First, because they are different people, but also because they may have a different function in the workplace. They understand what motivates their team as a unit, and what motivates the individuals that make up that team. And since they understand that the foundation of leadership is service, they put their energy into the improvement of their teams.

Notice that I didn't say anything about titles and reporting structure. Good leaders don't have to have a reporting structure to lead a team. They lead best from a place of influence. The best leaders influence others to move in a particular direction. Even better than that, they inspire others and leave an impact on the team as a whole, as well as the individuals on the team. Finally, to me the best leaders develop the next round of leaders—and they will remember that leader who inspired or shaped their thinking, ultimately helping them better understand how they themselves lead.

The military is a great place to learn and display leadership. While I did not serve in the military, I grew up in it (my father served 20 years in the United States Air Force). As a result, I can appreciate Lieutenant Colonel Daniel E. Harris's service. I learned a lot about leadership from growing up in the military and use many of those skills in the teams I lead today.

In *On Guard: The Four Pillars of Leadership* you have in your hands a detailed manual of the life of someone who learned to lead himself. This knowledge and experience helped LTC Daniel E. Harris lead others. There were prominent people and leaders who had an influence on his life and career, and he, in turn, is utilizing that to benefit others.

When I refer to solid leadership and good teamwork, I can assure you that LTC Harris exemplifies both of these attributes. *On Guard* gets into the nuts and bolts of how he learned and applied certain approaches throughout his illustrious career. And now, with this book, you can use them throughout yours, too, regardless of where you are in your journey. Enjoy the ride!

—Dr. Lamar Blackwell
Research & Development Scientist and Team Leader

PROLOGUE

Hitting Home

"When we are no longer able to change a situation, we are challenged to change ourselves." — Viktor Frankl

When terrorists flew planes into the World Trade Center in New York City, the Pentagon outside of Washington, D.C., and a field in Pennsylvania, I took it personally. I felt like I had let my country down. As a member of the National Guard, it was our job to protect our country. And yet we had been caught "off guard."

The End of the Innocence

Because I grew up so close to the Twin Towers, I knew people who were affected by their collapse.

I later found out that Captain Dan McNally was there and what follows is his recollection of that chaotic day. It was gleaned from a compilation of over 500 testimonies, entitled *Voices of 9.11: Here is New York* (Daniel L. McNally), recorded in 2002 and 2003.

He was a New York City police detective assigned to the bomb squad. September 11, 2001 was his day off. He was in the process of waking up when he heard the first plane hit the North Tower from his Manhattan home. He thought it was a transformer exploding over at the local Con Edison plant, so he went into the living room and turned on the local news. The TV started broadcasting that a plane had struck the World Trade Center. He was watching the newscast when he saw the second plane hit.

At that point McNally was able to flag down a security patrol at his housing complex and get a ride over to the bomb squad office located in Greenwich Village. There he hooked up with other members of the NYC bomb squad, including Detective Steve "Ziggy" Berberich and Detective Claude (Daniel) Richards, and they were told to mobilize on Vesey Street and Church, which is at the northeast corner of the World Trade Center complex.

Mobilization

As they approached the mobilization point, they saw the South Tower collapse and spew out quite a bit of debris.

McNally looked down Vesey and saw a lone New York City Police sergeant in the middle of Vesey Street, trying to direct people off of the plaza to the escalators that went from the street level up to the plaza level. The sergeant was alone and McNally, Richards and Berberich, plus Detective Mike Oldmixon and Joe Dolan from the bomb squad, ran down and started to assist.

Going up onto the plaza after the first building collapsed, McNally would later recall that "the North Tower was fully engulfed, and she was peeling off parts of her facade—pieces of glass were coming down, pieces of light and trim work that surrounded the building were collapsing. It was a very dangerous place to be."

People who had somehow made it from the South Tower as well as people who had been in the North Tower, had to find a way to traverse the plaza. First responders cleared an area for them to walk through, including clearing debris away from the escalators and directing people to a safe way out onto Vesey Street and north of Church onto Broadway.

McNally and his colleagues connected with a few Emergency Service Unit (ESU) officers at that time. They had air packs and rappelling harnesses on—all their safety gear. What they didn't have were backboards. McNally and Richards asked them what they needed. These guys had been climbing stairs for the last half hour or so. The weight of their safety equipment was really taking a toll. So McNally and Richards ran down to the ambulances that were staging up by Broadway and Vesey and secured a backboard to carry those immobilized.

Building Six

McNally and Detective Richards were then going to act as a litter (stretcher) carrier to get people off the plaza. The North Tower was fully engulfed and an evacuation had been called for the tower. They were able to clear the plaza of pedestrians. As rescue workers came out of the towers, the members of the bomb squad were able to draw them to the overhang of Building Six, the U.S. Customs House, and give them safe passage up to Vesey Street, off the plaza and out of the area.

That's when they hooked up with Emergency Services officers Mark DeMarco, Billy Buery and John D'Allara. There were two other officers from the Emergency Services of the Port Authority, and McNally and company said they were going to sweep through the lobby of Building Six and push people out onto West Street to clear the area. As they were going through Building Six, they could hear the North Tower falling above them. It was an extremely loud noise.

Later they were told it took eight seconds for the North Tower to come down. McNally said he probably remembered about five seconds of it. When the North Tower was coming down, the building they were in shook. So, by instinct, they hugged the wall. McNally and the four guys in front of him held onto each other, front to back, until after the collapse. There were three guys no more than 15 feet behind him; John D'Allara, Claude Richards, and an Emergency Services officer, Sergeant Mike Curtin.

When the tower came down, they thought they were trapped in Building Six. Parts of the ceiling fell on top of them and the pressure pushed McNally's right shoulder to a wall. But they held onto each other tightly. He remembered holding onto the air bottle of the guy in front of him as tightly as possible.

Time for a Quick Prayer

McNally said, "You had just about enough time to get out a quick prayer." His prayer, as well as those of many other survivors as he later discovered, was, "Dear God, if you're going to take me, take me fast." He then braced for a piece of steel going through his back. He prepared for the end. But it didn't come. The building collapse had stopped.

But then what ensued was even more horrifying: Thick pulverized concrete dust blacked out the sun and the light. "It was so heavy that you couldn't breathe," he later said. He had a particulate mask on but it clogged up right away. So there was no air—and not being able to see or breathe was particularly terrifying.

They knew they were in trouble, so they reversed their course and tried to go out the same way they entered the building. Mark DeMarco was in front, and Billy Buery held on so tight McNally had black and blue prints of his hands on his rib cage and chest the next day. But he was grateful that he did hold on.

Our Darkest Hour

Mark DeMarco had a flashlight and a respirator and was going to lead the men out of the collapsed portion of the building. But they could only go about 10-15 feet. The North Tower's collapse pancaked the building they were in and pushed the roof down into the sub-basement. With that, Sergeant D'Allara, Sergeant Curtin and Detective Richards met their maker. It was terrifying.

McNally and the remaining guys couldn't go anywhere. They had to wait until enough sediment fell out of the sky so they could see. They had no footing and no floors underneath them. The sediment was so heavy—but it wasn't smoke. It was pulverized concrete and glass, office furniture, lighting fixtures and possibly people falling out of the air. It took two to three minutes for it all to fall, which must've seemed like an eternity.

That's when McNally saw a civilian who had a very powerful flashlight. He took the flashlight and went back to look for his fellow officers. The thought of losing his fellow law enforcement officers was excruciating. He and Claude "Danny" Richards had gone to the Police Academy together and had been partners for about 15 years on the bomb squad. He had also worked with John D'Allara as a cop in the Bronx before McNally went to work with the bomb squad.

Because enough sediment had fallen out of the air, fires that would continue for months had started in the pit that was caused by the collapse of the North Tower. He looked down into this "abyss," and he couldn't see the edges of it. It was so wide and big that there was no way for him to get around it and there was no way for him to get down there. Even looking down, he was looking into a hole that was 45 feet deep.

They finally got out on the Western side of the plaza. McNally couldn't remember if DeMarco had shot the windows out or not. Luckily, two other emergency services officers heard their call for help.

A Devastating Blow

"Oh good, the firemen are here to get us off the plaza, which was about a 30 foot drop," he recollected. But then he looked slightly to the south toward the north traverse bridge that went from the financial center to the World Trade Center, and noticed it had collapsed onto a fire truck. And then he realized all the devastation along West Street; fire trucks were crushed and some of them were burning. The firemen along West Street had just survived the same collapse that McNally and company had endured. And yet, with the help of the Emergency Services officers and the firefighters, they were able to get ladders up so they could extract themselves from a very dangerous area.

When the North Tower collapsed, it sheared the facades off adjacent buildings and parts of their facades were still collapsing and hitting the ground. Five of the group he was with got down. He stayed. He knew where his partner, Danny Richards, was in relation to the lobby and he didn't want to leave him and didn't know how he could report him.

That's when he saw five firemen literally marching down West Street. They were fresh. They had just arrived on the scene. And they were determined. They went in the same location from which McNally and his men had emerged. McNally said, "Okay, listen, this is where we were... this is what I think is going on. This is where I think these guys are." And they went in and they looked. But they couldn't find them.

Fortunately, though, they found a fire lieutenant on the plaza level who was kind of knocked out and was buried under some light debris. He was okay.

And then, that was it. That was the end of the collapse. McNally tells people that don't know him about that day. He tells them he was in the company of very, very good men. The guys from the bomb squad, NYPD and Emergency Services Unit are probably the strongest men he knows, ever knew, or will ever know.

Because he had worked the first World Trade Center bombing in 1993, he had a guestimate as to the size of the damage of this thing.

They recovered the bodies of the lost officers the following spring. Richards was found on Good Friday, Valera on Ascension Thursday (40 days after Easter), and Curtin between those two periods of time. Recovery crews had tried to go down there prior to that but it was physically impossible because of the amount of tonnage that was on top of the men.

***

Bonkers in Yonkers

"Yes, peace can and must be won, to save the world from the terrible destruction of World War III." – Paul Robeson

The Neil Simon play *Lost in Yonkers,* although a comedy, touched on such surprisingly dark themes as survival at any cost, the dysfunctional family, the need to feel loved by a parent, and mental illness. My September 11, 2001—although not nearly as harrowing as Dan McNally's, and many others who displayed extreme leadership and lost their lives—was, perhaps, just as surreal. I have no doubt that nearly everyone reading this has their own personal recollection of the day.

That Tuesday started as it often did for me, waking at 0400 for the two and a half hour commute from Northeast Pennsylvania to New York. The sky was azure blue as I left my home in the Pocono Mountains and it seemed like any other day on the planet. However, while I was leaving my compound, which is a gated community, I caught on the television in the guard station a glimpse of the first tower after it was hit. I briefly spoke with the security officer, then pointed my car south on Route 196 onto Route 611 South, then east on I-80 toward the George Washington Bridge, which connects New Jersey with New York City.

As I headed east on Interstate 80 to the Interstate 280 split, I couldn't get the news fast enough. Approaching the bridge, it was evident that it was closed. I said to myself that I would figure out how to get to my office when I got to the bridge. I had to reach my office. My family was relatively safe, but I needed to get to the Armory.

I had a sick feeling in my gut and I felt heaviness and uncertainty when I heard that the three main area airports—JFK, LaGuardia, and

Newark—were shut down, with no incoming or outgoing flights. I said to myself, "This is real and very serious."

Because I was wearing my uniform, they let me cross over into Manhattan. Several people—strangers, realizing I had special dispensation to proceed in my vehicle—jumped into my car, pleading that I carry them across the bridge. I was more than willing to oblige. As we drove across the bridge with 1010 WINS News on the radio, it was a quiet ride with all eyes looking south across the Hudson River, at the towers, with smoke rising from the top.

As I prepared to exit the bridge onto 178th Street, I broke the silence by announcing that I was headed north on 9A into Yonkers. One person said, "You boys are going to be busy, good luck," and I remember saying, "Yeah, we'll be alright, you all be careful." Somehow the silent ride across the bridge and digesting the attack on our homeland had bonded us together. We were Americans and we had been attacked. And we were responsible for each other now.

New York City

When we got over to New York, my riders got out at 178th and Broadway, thanked me profusely and headed into the subway for the A-train downtown. I turned north on Broadway to search out my next entrance onto 9A North to head toward the Armory in Yonkers.

When I arrived at the Armory, I opened the building and shut off the alarms. I was the Battalion Administrative Officer (AO), the senior full-time military officer representing the command who worked with the civilian building superintendent in that particular armory. I contacted headquarters in Latham, New York, and the Engineering Brigade Headquarters in Buffalo, and told them I was on the ground and in the building.

Then I saw the National Guard go to work—as it had done countless times before. I remembered numerous other instances such as the call up for Operation Desert Storm, the ice storm that hit the New York North Country dairy farms, the prison strike, etc. Soldiers, realizing their civilian workday was shot and they would most likely be called up, started making their way into the building and changing into their uniforms. Battalion Command Sergeant Major (CSM) Joe Boledovic arrived, affirming, "It's a mess out there."

I told him I was watching the news, listening to the radio, and keeping tabs on the email string with the latest updates, and that I had also been in touch with headquarters. The great thing about a headquarters unit like this one was that many of the soldiers were senior non-commissioned officers (NCOs) as well as officers who require no supervision. They go straight to work without being told what to do. On that day, they simply went into gear and began to exercise their battle drills and execute the battle rhythm. The CSM provided oversight as the soldiers prepared their vehicles and fuel, packed overnight duffel bags, and secured government credit cards, safety equipment, and other classes of supplies. The other full-time soldiers like Sergeant First Class Patterson, Staff Sergeant Hagen, and Sergeant First Class Sanchez manned the phones with me and handled other administrative functions while monitoring what was going on.

With each passing hour, there seemed to be an escalation. Whenever we thought the worst was over, it got worse. No one seemed to know which way was up.

Since we weren't sure if there were going to be crowds rioting in the streets or what would take place next, my first order of business was to secure the armory. We kept weapons there and they needed to be secured.

Reassurance Was Necessary

Later that morning, something very profound happened to me. There was still quite a bit of activity going on when I went outside to walk around and take a look to see how things were going. It was then that I noticed one of the neighbors—an older woman—across the street.

I slowed down to engage her and she said to me, "You know, you soldiers all look pretty safe in your armory. What about us?" I looked around and realized, and understood, her fear. We had guards with radios in Humvee vehicles at the entrance to the parking lots. We also had guards at all entrances and exits of the building, and we even had two soldiers on the roof with binoculars and radios. The civilian-led agencies, police, fire and Emergency Services were very busy (to say the least) and this poor civilian lady had very little confidence in terms of her protection. I told her, "Ma'am, I have weapons inside the building.

We need to secure them. That was the reason for the heavy presence. You will be okay and we all will be okay. Don't worry."

This exchange really left an impression on me. It occurred to me that now that the towers had collapsed and we were hearing news of planes crashing in Shanksville, Pennsylvania and into the Pentagon, with talk about another one hitting the White House, it was also our responsibility to reassure our people of their personal safety.

That Afternoon

By that afternoon and evening, everything had stopped. The investigation was in full swing. We prepared our trucks and Humvees for the drive downtown.

The 342nd FSB (Forward Support Battalion (FSB) was structured under the old Army of Excellence combat service support unit concept. Typically an FSB provides service and sustainment support to three maneuver brigades in divisions: an Armor Brigade with tanks, an Infantry Brigade with Bradley fighting vehicles and the mounted and dismounted Infantry Brigade, and the Artillery Brigade (we call them the big guns consisting of howitzers, paladins, and such).

Collectively these three brigades, known as "killers," received their sustainment support from an FSB. Because they're normally engaged in the fight, the FSB with its robust capability in its C-level II medical company, its B-heavy maintenance company with small maintenance teams, is present with them and provides their classes of supplies. That includes everything—from food, fuel, and big and small bullets to maintenance for their vehicles, parts, and supplies, with the ability to purchase commercial off-the shelf items. It is a huge logistical element that has a command and control element for oversight of the FSB and quartermaster element.

We took this structure and converted it to working on the streets of New York. We already had lots of equipment. From our headquarters in Yonkers, we moved soldiers down toward the site. We also notified the armory on Bedford Avenue in Brooklyn, headed up by Miguel Castillo, a good friend of mine. He and his team moved over to Manhattan.

We set up camp underneath FDR Drive, right around the old Fulton Fish Market. For the rest of the time, that's where we worked.

Supplies came from all over the Tri-State area: New York, Connecticut, and New Jersey. Whenever supplies were donated by stores such as Old Navy, Home Depot, and others, the FSB received, inventoried, and then prepared them for distribution to the citizens of New York City.

Approaching Ground Zero

After staying at our headquarters in Yonkers for hours on end, it finally came time for me to drive downtown and approach the site. All of a sudden, it became very personal. I couldn't believe the carnage! It literally looked like the end of the world.

The gravity of the situation was horrific. The number of emergency vehicles seemed limitless. People were walking around in a daze, many of them looking like zombies. Most were trying to locate loved ones. A cloud of dust and smoke enveloped the area. The smell of burning metal was in the air and couldn't be shaken. It was a surreal first day.

Subsequently, after that, people left notes on buildings and on barrier walls. They hung pictures all over creation with contact numbers and addresses, suggesting that you please notify the individual who wrote it if you saw the person described. There were post-its everywhere. It was pretty grave.

The Transition

We worked there for a number of months before the state called off the mission and turned it over completely to the civilian agencies to do their work.

September 11, 2001, was a day when most New Yorkers, as well as people far and wide, got up and went to work as they did many other days prior. However, many of them never returned home. From that day on, things would never be the same.

The event occurred and we had no control over it. However, how we dealt and reacted to it, how we packaged our leadership, demonstrated and delivered it, how the National Guard responded and remained on guard, was something we could control—and we responded well.

In any engagement, there is a critical time and place that the leader needs to identify and place him- or herself in order for the engagement to be successful. President Bush found that critical moment and placed himself there effectively, as did Mayor Giuliani and Governor Pataki.

I identified that sense of leadership by walking around and responding to our neighbors in Yonkers, and many leaders demonstrated their leadership well that day. They were present with their teams and they were seen among the people providing direction, reassuring them, explaining the vision for the way ahead; caring, consoling, sharing, and letting people know that they would be all right. Leading people is a love affair of the heart and the head.

***

Leadership in Action

"I'd rather see a sermon than hear one any day." —Anonymous

Once again, I saw leadership in action immediately after 9.11. Not only was Dan McNally my hero, but in the face of serious challenges, other people stepped up, too.

Leadership on the Move

Mayor Rudy Giuliani was all over the city, assuring people that everything was going to be okay. His leadership at this time was remarkable. Ironically, Giuliani was writing a book on leadership when 9.11 happened. It was about two-thirds to three-quarters done when the attack occurred. He had been doing his best to take on challenges his whole life.

One thing that Giuliani did, after the attacks of September 11, was to go home (it was the twelfth by then) and lay out his clothes for the next day, just in case he got called in the middle of the night and had to rush out. He learned that from Fiorello La Guardia, another former mayor of New York City.

He then noticed a book on his nightstand that had recently come out about Churchill. He'd already read the first two or three chapters. He picked it up and read more, putting the attack into perspective. The British suffered much worse, he realized, getting slammed day in and day out in 1940 during the Battle of Britain. Ironically, he'd been thinking about the Battle of Britain that day. If they could get through it, he thought, then we can get through this.

The Attack

On the morning of September 11, Giuliani had just finished breakfast with several other politicians when he was told about a twin-engine plane hitting the World Trade Center (WTC). As they drove to the site, they could see the fire. And then the second plane hit. Once he realized it was a terrorist attack, the mayor tried to get Washington on the phone for air support and he tried to reach the governor to involve the National Guard.

Soon after arriving on the scene, he saw a guy jump from the 101st floor. That really affected him. Fortunately, they had two command posts—because one of them was in the WTC. The one at the trade center had to be reestablished, so they decided on the Police Academy.

Then Giuliani and Governor Pataki decided to work together with their respective entities, and that was a good decision. Good leaders communicate tirelessly with and among the people. For days to come, he and the governor made joint decisions. When the mayor made a decision, the governor would know about it, and vice versa. That way there wouldn't be finger pointing, which is the last thing you want in a crisis. They each told their staff: "You'd better not fight. This is bigger than all of us. Everybody is going to get the blame, and everybody is going to get the credit." That emphasis from the two leaders framed the climate for both the governor and the mayor's staff and that helped a great deal.

In dealing with panic and anger, Giuliani drew from his father's advice: "Whenever you're in an emergency, remain calm. Because the only way you're going to figure out how to get out of it is if you're calm. If you get very emotional, you'll just be banging into walls. If you remain calm, you'll be able to think your way out of it." He still struggles with the anger. He told President Bush that when he found bin Laden, he would like to be the one to execute him.

Leading Up to the Event

Mayor Giuliani had done some amazing things prior to 9.11. A former prosecutor, he'd taken on crime by starting with small matters and working his way up. He'd inherited a city with 1,900 to 2,000 murders a year and 12,000 felonies a week. It was the crime capital of America. People were afraid to go to New York.

He started by taking on the squeegee men—the guys who went up to vehicles at traffic lights and accosted drivers. He found out that a quarter of them had warrants for violent crimes. The constant pressure on them from the police made it so that accosting drivers wasn't worth it to them anymore. The mission was accomplished and the squeegee men went away. People saw that and realized that even though it was a small step, it worked. Good leaders develop and build on small wins one at a time. Small wins are easy to achieve. Big wins take much more effort.

One success led to another. They applied the same pressure to graffiti and to subway theft—where people would jump over turnstiles and not pay their fees. They applied it to minor concerns first, all the while working on bigger things. And it gave people the assurance that progress was taking place.

The result was a two-thirds decline in murder. People hadn't seen rates that low since the '60s.

He Had a Platform and Led from the Front

Giuliani realized that he had been elected because things were horrible. The city was a mess. Crime was most visible. He was the first Republican mayor in 25 years.

Good leaders always lead from the front. As mayor, he was omnipresent, on television and radio all the time. He had his own radio show and a town hall meeting once a month, nearly 100 of them while he was the mayor—in every community. So, he was accessible.

When the WTC was attacked, he had the bandwidth, the platform, and the channels of distribution, so to speak, to get the word out and to connect with people. And that's what he did.

People couldn't help but notice. It was reassuring. Leadership was on full display, front and center, at a very crucial time for our great country. Say what you want about Giuliani now, but after 9.11, he was a leader of legendary proportions.

***

PART 1

MY JOURNEY

Most people know the pros and cons of an enlisted soldier. The cons are that the pay is pitiful, the hours are long, you're away from your family and you're not exactly treated like an adult.

The pros, on the other hand, are that you receive benefits: medical, food, education, and retirement. You get job training and experience. You will travel and get in tremendous shape (there's quite a bit of running, and you have access to weights, tracks and trails, etc.). And, being a veteran, you have inherited a significant level of discipline, the first of which is LISTENING: beeps, knocks, clicks, and voice commands become important things to listen for. You also know good leadership when you see it—and can demonstrate it as well.

Many people know that the military's chief goal is to fight and win America's wars, with the overall mission of U.S. security and peace. A good number of them also know that the armed forces comprise the following branches: Air Force and Air Force Reserve, Air National Guard, Army and Army Reserve, Army National Guard, Coast Guard and Coast Guard Reserve, Marine Corps and Marine Corps Reserve, and the Navy and the Navy Reserve.

My tour of duty was served in the Army National Guard (ARNG).

CHAPTER 1
Readiness

"The readiness is all." –Hamlet

A story is told about a job opening for a Morse code operator. The interview for the job was held in an office with a reception area. An applicant arrived in the reception area to find two other applicants sitting there waiting. A few minutes later, the person who got there last stood up and walked right into the hiring manager's office. About five minutes later, the hiring manager and the guy who had walked in came out and the manager announced, "Thank you for coming but the job has been filled. You may go home now."

The other applicants were miffed. They said, "That's not fair! He got here after us and he wasn't even summoned into your office!" The hiring manager said, "All the time you've been sitting here, that teletype machine has been rattling off Morse code. One of the messages said, 'If you understand this message, come inside the office. The job is yours.'" He went on, "A Morse code operator has to always be on the alert. This young man heard the message and understood it. Therefore, the job is his."

My Story

In February 1977, when I was 15 years old, my mother, Elvira, younger brother Peter-Francis, and younger sister Frances and I emigrated from Liberia, Western Africa, to join my father in the United States. Dad had emigrated in 1970 and attended Fordham University in Bronx, New York, and Union Theological Seminary, to obtain his Doctor of Divinity and Metaphysics. We moved to the U.S. and lived in Dad's one-bedroom apartment on St. Nicholas Avenue near 150th

Street in Harlem, New York. In April 1977, we moved and settled in Staten Island, in an area between the Park Hill and Stapleton neighborhood projects. Thus began my American journey.

That fall, in October, Mr. William (Dick) Ryan, my Curtis High School biology teacher said, "An American is not a person, but rather, an American is a way of thinking. It is one who thinks of being good, compassionate, responsible, hardworking, and free." The words resonated with me as I smiled and thought to myself, "I must have always been an American." Over the remainder of my high school years, Mr. Ryan and I grew to be close as I learned much from him and many other great Americans.

In March 2014, there was a serious outbreak of Ebola in Liberia. When the disease first hit, medical practitioners thought it was malaria (very common there), thus leading to many doctors becoming infected. Before the virus, the country, which had a population of 4.5 million at the time, had only 50 doctors—and fewer in the neighboring country, Sierra Leone. Liberia's health system had been severely depleted because of a civil war, which ended in 2003. So medical personnel were hard to come by.

Because of the fact that people thought it was malaria, the disease had several months to spread before it was diagnosed as Ebola. When it was realized, some airlines suspended all flights between Liberia and many other countries, even within Africa (cases were also discovered in Mali, Nigeria, Senegal, and Guinea, but to a lesser extent). By August of that year, teams of workers were trying to bury bodies. Locals quarreled with them because the body of a patient who died from Ebola is highly contagious in the days following the death. Wild dogs were digging up bodies and becoming carriers of the disease.

People were protesting and a mob of residents from my hometown of Monrovia, an impoverished section of the country, incited a riot at the local Ebola clinic, looting its supplies. People feared this would lead to a widespread outbreak. By October, there was an exponential growth of cases. People panicked and many concluded that the virus was out of control.

Healthcare establishments were overwhelmed and couldn't take care of the influx of patients. Hordes of infected people were being turned away from treatment centers. In mid-October, the National

Guard and reservists from the U.S. military arrived. By early November, there were over 6,500 cases and nearly 3,000 deaths in Liberia.

The Centers for Disease Control and Prevention (CDC) devised an integration strategy, combining isolation and treatment with community behavior change—such as safe burial practices, case finding, and contact tracing. This helped a great deal. In mid-November, Liberian President Ellen Johnson Sirleaf announced she was lifting the state of emergency in the country, following the decrease in the number of new cases.

Still There

The outbreak persisted. In January of the following year, it seemed to be confined to two counties of Liberia. In February, Liberia opened its land borders. On May 9 of that year, after 42 days passed with no new cases of Ebola being reported, the country declared itself "Ebola free."

However, several cases have broken out since, prompting Liberia to declare additional "Ebola free" days (September 3, 2015; January 14, 2016; and June 9, 2016).

While progress is ongoing, I'd like to take this opportunity to tell you about my interaction with leaders in my travels since the outbreak.

Three West African countries were mostly affected by the Ebola virus: Sierra Leone, Liberia (heavily hit), and Guinea (much less). When I met with leaders from these three countries, I asked them the question, "What is the plan for the next Ebola?" This is something a leader needs to think about to develop mitigating steps. In my estimation, that's a big part of what leadership is.

Some people may think my standards are too high, but I was expecting more from the leaders I met. What lessons did we learn from this? How can we use this experience to improve people's lives? Maybe you develop mitigating measures. Or you ask yourself, "How do we minimize that?" So, instead of 300 people getting killed, it is only 50. Whatever the case, you're going to be impacted.

So, when you ask the question, "What is the plan for the next Ebola?" and you get nothing, it is clear we have work to do. There WILL be another Ebola. It could be a famine, a fire, a flood or another pandemic. As this book goes to press, we are in the midst of the

COVID-19 outbreak, which is infecting the entire world! So, obviously, there are additional "Ebolas." When it hits and you say, "Oh my, we have a problem!" then you have failed—because everyone can see there is a problem. It is too late!

The genius lies in being able to recognize what could happen 30, 60, 90, 120 days, or even a year (or years) ahead of time.

The problem in many places around the world is leadership (or lack thereof). There's not that sense of looking and leaning forward, and being "on guard" to anticipate problems and make decisions in a timely manner. Leaders also create and develop the vision for the way forward. They help establish the path for the future. They can't establish that path if they aren't paying attention to what is coming.

In the ensuing chapters, I intend to lay out my experiences and understanding of when leadership was extraordinary and when it was dreadful, and thus inspire the leader that lies within you. I have seen it play out—both ways—in some dire circumstances as well as in everyday life. After all, having served in the U.S. military for over three decades, I have had a front-row seat to the greatest show on earth: working, watching, observing, looking, and learning through a close-up view of people living out their lives.

Exactly What is Leadership?

Leadership is getting people to do what you want them to do in a timely manner without resorting to threats, intimidation, or humiliation. Followers have the obligation to dismiss anything that is illegal or immoral. Some may think leadership is a thankless task, and it is, because often it is not even recognized when it is done well. And when it is done poorly, when there's a dearth of it, or even when people simply don't like the leader or the way he or she is doing things, criticism abounds. Sometimes rightfully so. But often leadership is underappreciated, or simply unappreciated.

Some say leadership really only happens in a crisis. I beg to differ. Leadership is all around us, through us, and within us all the time. There are always opportunities to demonstrate leadership at every moment. Rev. Dr. Martin Luther King, Jr. once said, "The time is always right to do the right thing." That is because the time is always right to demonstrate leadership. Leaders do the "right thing," selflessly, always.

Leadership comes in all shapes and sizes. Daniel Goleman, author of *Emotional Intelligence,* wrote in an article entitled "Leadership That Gets Results" that there are six forms of leadership: authoritarian, paternalistic, democratic, laissez-faire, transactional, and transformational. Others simply say they know it when they see it.

I submit that courage, integrity, passion, and love are the four pillars or the foundation upon which all forms of leadership are built.

***

CHAPTER 2
Formative Years

"For evil to flourish, it only requires good men to do nothing."
—Simon Wiesenthal

While living in the U.S., I attended Curtis High School, operated by the New York City Department of Education. Curtis High, which was named after the American writer and public speaker George W. Curtis, is one of seven public high schools located in Staten Island. Our mascot was the Warrior.

While there, I became known as "The Science Guy" by my classmates because I participated in science fairs. I hung around the science department between classes, during lunch breaks, and after school before I ran track. I was always in the science department. I also worked there (non-paid), setting up the labs for chemistry, physics, and biology.

In my sophomore year, I met a teacher by the name of Mr. Caspar Sheiper. He was a very friendly man and mentor. He told me that many scientific papers were written in German and in order to understand them, I needed to learn German too. So I studied German in high school as well as later on in college.

The Big Apple

From the classrooms at Curtis, I could see the Statue of Liberty and the skyscrapers across the New York Harbor. On occasion, we would ride the Staten Island Ferry over into Manhattan and take the subway. Back then, subway cars in New York were appalling. They were dirty, graffiti-ridden, and they smelled badly—and many of them didn't even have working lights. I remembered riding in the dark subway cars a lot of the time.

In 1984, an incident took place that became a tipping point. Bernhard Goetz, who came to be known by the press as the "Subway Vigilante," shot and wounded four teenagers on a subway car in Manhattan. The episode sparked nationwide debate on such topics as race and crime in major cities, the legal limits of self-defense, and the extent to which citizens could rely on police to secure their safety.

The event came to symbolize the frustration New Yorkers had with high crime rates at that time. I didn't have to look very far to realize that there was a need for leadership everywhere, from Liberia to the local subway station. Before long, the "broken windows theory" would be introduced to New Yorkers, which states that visible signs of crime, anti-social behavior, and disorder creates an environment that encourages further crime and disorder, including serious crime.

It was right around this time that I started to become passionate about leadership.

The Militia

Knowing that one person can make a difference, in 1988, at age 26, I joined the National Guard and became known by my drill sergeants and fellow trainees in Fort Leonard Wood (Missouri) as the "Smart Old Man (SOM)" in Basic Combat Training (BCT) and Advanced Individual Training (AIT). I was in the reserves, working one weekend a month and two weeks a year. The "Institute" (the New York State Institute for Basic Research in Developmental Disabilities) and Columbia University—where I worked as a research assistant in the Black Building for most of the '80s—were very supportive of my service.

Before I left Liberia, my grandfather, Pedro, told my brother and me, "I don't know where you boys will end up. But whatever country you live in, serve her in her military." That always stuck with me.

The National Guard (from the French *Garde nationale*) was originally a group of civilians, farmers, shopkeepers, and merchants who, at a moment's notice, took up arms in defense of their way of life, whether it was against the British or fighting on the frontier.

They were founded on December 13, 1636, when the first militia regiments in North America were organized in Massachusetts. The National Guard predates the Army. The Air National Guard (which is the branch of service that George W. Bush served) was founded in 1947. Likewise, it predates the Air Force.

The oldest Army National Guard units are the 101st Engineer Battalion, the 101st Field Artillery Regiment, the 181st Infantry Regiment, and the 182nd Infantry Regiment, all of the Massachusetts Army National Guard. They take orders from both the governor of the state that they are affiliated with, as well as the president. And they receive benefits from both the state and the federal government.

Presidents who served in the Army National Guard include George Washington, Thomas Jefferson, James Madison, James Monroe, Andrew Jackson, William Henry Harrison, John Tyler, James Polk, Millard Fillmore, Franklin Pierce, James Buchanan, Abraham Lincoln, Andrew Johnson, Ulysses S. Grant, Rutherford B. Hayes, James Garfield, Chester Arthur, Benjamin Harrison, William McKinley, Teddy Roosevelt, and Harry S. Truman. Babe Ruth also served in the Army National Guard.

Because members of the National Guard simultaneously work in the private sector, they also know about civilian life and can therefore better relate to those they are helping.

I have learned from a variety of leaders throughout my life. One of them was the aforementioned Captain Dan McNally, who had worked for the NYPD on the bomb squad as a civilian and served in the Army National Guard. Captain McNally was my Headquarters and Headquarters Company (HHC) Commander of the 102nd Engineer Battalion located on 168th and Fort Washington in New York City.

Captain Dan McNally was an Excellent Role Model

I was enlisted. I started out as a private first class (an E-3, just below a specialist). Captain Dan McNally and First Sergeant Richard Kolodkin put me in Officer Candidate School (OCS). They saw something in me, and I am forever grateful. They signed my documentation and told me I needed to go to OCS.

I liked Captain McNally's leadership style. He was a strong man, focused on the Army's work. He was about doing the right thing. He was clear about the mission and what needed to be done and he set about doing it. His philosophy was, "Do what your gut tells you to do. Do the right thing."

Because he and First Sergeant Kolodkin had been with the NYPD, they knew how to read people very well without having to say a whole lot. I once saw Captain McNally go toe-to-toe with a major. Captain McNally was the company commander at the time and was in charge of all things administrative: documentation, physical fitness qualifications, weapons and night vision qualifications, nuclear, biological and chemical certification, and many other metrics that had to be ticked off.

The major didn't want to go to the firing range. McNally, although he was outranked, held his ground. They both dug in their heels. Captain McNally told the major that he was going to give him a 0, an unsatisfactory mark and the colonel would be notified. His position was, "Even though you outrank me, administratively, I am the company commander." And he was right. After all, if he didn't do what he was supposed to do and sign the attendance roster, even the colonel wouldn't get paid. Anyway, the major, who had been sitting in the barracks, eventually stormed out to the firing range.

Afterwards, Captain McNally said to me, "You know, Mr. Harris, leadership is not a popularity contest." Later on he laughed and said, "I am in the unenviable position where no one likes me. The black guys think I'm a racist and the white guys think I'm a bigot. I'm in the middle. And I don't care."

Captain McNally was not afraid to be independent. Many in the Guard can be very parochial and cliquish. Captain Dan McNally was neither of those. He didn't get into cliques.

My MOS in a Nutshell

One of the unique features about citizen soldiers and the Guard is that, under normal circumstances, things operate under Title 32 of the U.S. Code of the Reserves, where the governor is the commander in chief. But, on some occasions, when needed (e.g., during a national crisis), it operates under Title 10, where the president is the commander in chief. A prime example would be activating the reserves for war.

My Military Occupational Specialty (MOS) was 12B Army Combat Engineer as an enlisted service member and I branched as a 21A Combat Engineer Officer when I received my commission as a second lieutenant. The primary job of the Army combat engineers is to supervise, serve, and assist as a member of a unit when tackling rough terrain in combat situations. Army combat engineers leverage their expertise in general engineering, mobility and counter mobility, and survivability.

Some of my duties included building fighting positions, floating bridges, creating obstacles, detecting mines and other explosives, and placing and detonating explosives, just to name a few. I learned much about the fundamentals of leadership in my training and working as an Army combat engineer.

In my first full time job in the military, I was a Battalion Administrative Officer (AO) in a Forward Support Battalion. Typically, the AO is the senior ranking officer in the facility or installation in charge of the full-time staff and is responsible for the daily operation of the battalion. In this role, Captain Dan McNally's words of wisdom resonated with me often when he said, "As a leader you must always do the right thing and you never have to worry about anything."

He would then say, "...and if the whole damn thing comes crashing down when you were trying to do the right thing, don't worry. That's why we have investigations. They will investigate and if your efforts were sincere, honest, and genuine, you will be vindicated."

Wear the Uniform

As a leader you must always be honest with your team members. If you are not, they will see right through you like a chain-link fence—and you will be ineffective. My greatest enjoyment and satisfaction in my role as AO and officer was when I asked civilians—young men and women—to raise their right hand to take the oath to enlist in front of the flag. At the end of swearing them in and as I proceeded to shake their hand, I reminded them that the Army was paying them to wear the uniform and not necessarily to do the job. So always wear the uniform proudly.

You see, the Army can get anyone to do its work, but it cannot get anybody to wear the uniform. Effective leaders also wear a uniform and the fabric of the uniform is made of credibility, honesty, hard work, and compassion. These must permeate the fabric, or else the leader will be ineffective.

The basic foundation for being an effective leader is to be a good listener. I think that listening is slightly more important in leading than speaking. Listening is often overlooked and marginalized in the communication process. It involves controlling the ego and exercising self-control. During listening you can take in, process and analyze, make associations, and arrive at a conclusion. This is not the case when speaking. You learn a lot more when you're listening than when you are speaking. Listening is the key to alertness.

In a message, retired General Martin Dempsey included the following quote from Winston Churchill: "Courage is what it takes to stand up and speak. Courage is also what it takes to sit down and listen." Dempsey continued to say that, "Leadership is sensing what the organization needs: words can matter, so can silence; prominence can matter, so can deference."

Leading is Different from Managing

It is no secret that organizations spend billions of dollars each year to have their executives manage more effectively. But what is really needed in most organizations is not good management, but good leadership.

Likewise, institutions also spend billions of dollars each year to teach leadership. Despite the inordinate amount of money spent on the discipline, when it is needed, it is often lacking on a daily basis.

Are people born leaders—or do they learn it? We'll address these and many other issues around this key topic. I'll also provide my theory on leadership, most of it learned from over three decades in the military.

So, suit up and let's get going!

***

CHAPTER 3
Learning About Leadership

"An army of deer led by a lion is more to be feared than an army of lions led by a deer."—Philip of Macedonia

My first foray into leadership was while serving in the Guard in the late '90s. After serving as enlisted for a couple of years, I attended Officer Candidate School (OCS) and received a commission as a second lieutenant in June 1992. I started a civilian program called Inner City Institute (ICI). By this time, I was married with two children, Daniel Jr. and Antonia-Isis, and we lived on Gordon Street, opposite the Stapleton Projects. The Stapleton Projects and the area immediately surrounding it were very low income back then. Today, it's pretty commonplace to have computers and internet access, but back then, not everybody had access to computers or automation.

ICI itself was simply a space. The building I lived in and where ICI was headquartered previously had a gun and sporting goods store on the first level and living quarters on the top. We taught the elderly, the poor, single-parent families, and students about computers, giving many their only access to automation. This was back in the embryonic stages of the Internet. We taught things like WordPerfect, Word (3.1 at that time) and Quattro Pro. I received gifts of used computers and furniture through my network of friends and I bought a lot of other stuff from United Way and got it very inexpensively.

ICI sessions ran from 11 a.m. to 2 p.m. for the older folks. And then, at two o'clock, students began to come in who went to school but didn't have computers at home. They had no ways or means of getting computers where they lived. Many of these kids' families were single parents and received welfare assistance. ICI was open for them to come in and play around and do different things on the computers until 7 p.m. Then the adults would come in. The concept was, you'd get off work around 6 p.m., and then come in at 7 p.m. and work until around 11 p.m. They would work on resumes and make phone calls. They would do the things that we take to be commonplace today.

It was at that time that I realized that leaders are not only looking to solve problems, but they're always creating, always innovating, always making something. Also, for leaders, interacting with others is paramount.

Behind the Microscope

For the first 11 years of my military service, I was in the U.S. Army Reserve. As a civilian, I worked at Memorial Sloan-Kettering (MSK) Cancer Center as a research associate. This was after I had worked at the New York State Institute for Basic Research for nine years. While at MSK, I was participating in basic science research in head and neck cancers. Simultaneously, I was earning a Bachelor of Arts in History from City University of New York.

While at MSK, I wrote and published several papers. I studied the basic foundation of life (cells, proteins, and molecules). I worked with Stimson Schantz, MD, a brilliant surgeon, as well as with doctors John Strong, Peter Sacks, and Howard Savage. Dr. Savage had also worked at MD Anderson Cancer Center in Houston, Texas in the early '90s.

Part of my job was to obtain specimens by waiting in the operating room (OR) during surgery. Immediately upon removal of the cancer tumor from the patient, I obtained a small one-centimeter by one-centimeter piece of tissue and snap-froze the samples in liquid nitrogen, then returned to my laboratory for work. We isolated proteins, ran gel electrophoresis, examined biomarkers, and ran dose response curves to determine optimal doses for various chemotherapeutic agents. I got the opportunity to work on some fascinating experiments.

Looking at what configuration of chemotherapy agents worked optimally for patients of different demographics is intriguing work. We worked to determine why certain head and neck cancers behaved the way they did, given all of the variables of demographics, diet, environment, lifestyle, stress, sleep/rest cycles, and so forth and so on.

After nine years at MSK working for and with some very intelligent and practical doctors and staff, my take-away was simply this: the first and biggest responsibility of the medical team is to educate the individual patient and public as to whether they are in a high-risk category group or demographic that is susceptible to getting a particular disease based on their variables. Next was to treat patients when they manifest the disease. After providing the information, it must be left up to people to use their education as they see fit. I still don't understand why a cancer patient would sit outside of a cancer fighting hospital and smoke daily while in a wheelchair and connected to intravenous fluid. Nevertheless, I enjoyed science tremendously then and I still do today.

The medical doctors and the PhDs are the heads of the lab. When it came to writing papers, the doctor whose name will bring in the money goes first. Often, however, the lab associates (the second or third guy or gal down the totem pole) were the ones that pull all the levers and push all the buttons.

We would tease the cells from the tumor, grow them, and test various chemotherapeutic agents—cisplatin or Fluorouracil (5FU) or combinations thereof—to determine the optimum dose to kill the cancer cells. We would also extract the DNA from other cancer cells to examine various proteins and test different biomarkers. It became evident to me that each patient is different, even though they manifested the same disease, and how they got well depended on their individual variables, including risk category, genetic disposition, living and working environments as well as their level of daily stress, among other factors.

Diet also plays a huge role in this process. For example, the tumors of head and neck cancer patients whose diet consisted of foods with high amounts of curcumin or garlic responded poorly to cisplatin, but responded favorably to 5FU independently, yet trends still showed a synergistic response when we combined both chemotherapeutic agents.

To me, this is fascinating stuff! I have much respect and admiration for those who work in the medical profession. One of the things I learned and appreciated was the advantage of a research hospital versus a non-research hospital, where you don't have to wait four to five weeks for lab results to see whether your cancer is responding favorably or not to a particular drug regimen in a Stage IV cancer situation. Time is either your enemy or your friend.

Leadership Lessons

Keeping my head down and working hard, whether as a volunteer or a paid employee, put me in good stead for what was to come later in my career. I learned that people often size you up—and if they even sense that you've done what you're telling them to do, it gives you more authenticity and credibility.

***

CHAPTER 4
My Leadership Trajectory

"A leader is one who knows the way, goes the way and shows the way." —John Maxwell

Approximately 8,000 soldiers, airmen and women conduct domestic and homeland security/defense operations in the United States daily. They put their lives on the line for the good of the country.

In addition to security and peace, there's also the issue of illegal drug trafficking. The National Guard has a Counter Drug Program to support local law enforcement agencies. Terrorism is obviously also a key concern—as are riots. There needs to be Counter Terrorism as well as riot police.

The National Guard has a presence in 15 of the 16 Aerospace Alert Sites in the United States. They are in 2,600 communities in the states, territories, and the District of Columbia.

Army Strong

As I mentioned earlier, I served more than 30 years in the military—over 10 years in the Reserve and 20 years on active duty. I enlisted at age 26 and I was called the "Old Man." When you are in basic training, anyone above the age of 21 is considered old. My son Daniel had been born, I had a mortgage, and I had my name on several scientific papers that were published in reputable scientific journals.

Upon completing basic training and returning to my unit, my company commander Captain Dan McNally, as well as First Sergeant Richard Kolodkin, strongly supported and encouraged me to attend Officer Candidate School (OCS). I went to OCS at the Empire State Military Academy in New York.

In delineating my leadership positions in the military, I'll start with platoon leader and work all the way up to Battalion commander and my work with the Bureau and beyond. Although my military growth and professional development was linear, I don't necessarily think that my experience was. I don't know that I can describe it as a precise thought. This chapter deals with the overall trajectory of my career. Later I'll fill in the gaps. I think that format works best.

During my first command position I was a platoon leader. A platoon leader is typically a second lieutenant or a first Lieutenant who has a platoon sergeant that works with him/her. The Platoon Sergeant is typically the go-to person in the platoon and your number one person. I had about 60 soldiers under my command in my platoon. This role lasted for two years.

At any given time in the military, as an officer, you are either in command or you're serving on a staff. Typically, when someone rotates out of command, they rotate into a staff position. Serving in both staff and command positions significantly contributed to my leadership experience.

After platoon leader, I was assigned to several company-level staff positions such as Personnel, Operations and Training, Supply and Services (S&S) and Company Executive Officer. Following my company level staff assignments, my next leadership position was company commander. As a company commander, I was a senior first lieutenant. In that role, I had 170 soldiers in four platoons. In the company grade officer stint, I was responsible for not only the *collective* training of my soldiers, but also for managing, planning, resourcing, prioritizing, and decision-making. I was a company commander for four years.

Following company command time, I served in a number of battalion staff positions and, similar to my company level experience, my first battalion staff assignment was Personnel Officer in an administrative capacity called the S1 section (1 is for admin). In the civilian world that would be an HR-type appointment.

In that role I was responsible for all HR functions for the soldiers, including pay, family documentation, health/benefits, strength accountability, and management. I worked closely with the recruiters to fill vacancies and critical shortages as well as with the senior and junior company commanders on retention of their soldiers.

I spent a lot time managing excess soldiers on the Unit Manning

Rosters (UMR) and managing personnel during unit reorganizations. Every soldier must be accounted for and placed in a job that is compatible with their specialty, or I had to have a conversation with them about going back to school to be reclassified and retrained. As you might imagine, this caused a lot of retention issues.

But that was the easy work. The hard (and most important) work, I called the "crystal ball." You cannot afford to drop it or mess it up. When you drop it, like a crystal, it will shatter into a million pieces and you will never be able to fix it. This was the case with the monthly validation of the Unit Status Report (USR) and the quarterly USR build. This is a very important report for the Army because it deals with strength and readiness. Units can be decommissioned and units can be formed based on this report. I have seen commanders lose their jobs for not effectively and efficiently managing this report while others receive accolades for their due diligence and adept management of it.

As an S-1 officer, at the end of the day, this report kept me awake many nights. Following my time in the personnel administrative role, I then served as Battalion Operations Officer. In peacetime, the operations function is called "training" and when we're deployed in a theater of war, it is "operations." So typically, we will call the function Operations and Training.

In that capacity, I was responsible for a lot of the training and synchronizing and ensuring that the training supported and aligned with the overall mission of the battalion as well as the brigade and the division. Eventually, all of the training and operation pieces have to support the national strategy, which is at a very high level. This document is published by the commander in chief. While I am referring to my very low-level role in the organization, I always felt the importance of envisioning how my efforts and contributions fit and supported the big picture.

Following my stint as Battalion Operations Officer, I then moved into a Supply and Services (S&S) Officer role (again this is a staff position, so it's given an S designation). This basically entails coordinating and sourcing all of the beans and the bullets for the battalion.

Battalions

After I served in battalion staff positions, doing many of those same jobs in personnel, operations, and supply logistics at a higher level, I was then selected for command and I served my command time. Battalion command is characterized as having both responsibility and authority—in contrast to company command—where you have responsibility but no authority. This means that as a battalion commander, I had authority to exercise the Uniform Code of Military Justice (UCMJ) over my soldiers. I could deduct soldiers' pay, reduce soldiers in rank, and exercise other legal actions as directed under the UCMJ. This is serious business and it is one that I took very seriously. As a company commander, I had to direct those actions to my battalion commander. That is why we say a company commander has responsibility but no authority while a battalion commander has responsibility and authority.

At the battalion command level, I provided guidance, planning, managing and decision making, as well as resourcing and prioritizing, and had oversight and supervision of a staff of 57 full-time soldiers. That assignment lasted almost four years. I was assigned to battalion command in April 2010 and I rotated out in November 2013.

The Bureau

Following battalion command, again, out of command, I went back into staff. This time I was given an assignment at the National Guard Bureau in Virginia, located on George Mason Drive. There I worked as the Deputy Chief in logistics, on the Command Logistics Readiness Team (CLRT). This team has the responsibility of visiting subordinate elements of the National Guard Bureau Headquarters to assist and inspect for logistics readiness and check for compliance in policy and army regulations of all of the state National Guards. As you know, each state, according to our constitution, contains a militia and that militia is the National Guard. They have a lot of autonomy. But, in an effort to maintain standard, across-the-board, big army and active component Department of Defense (DoD), they establish this group to visit the states, territories, and the District of Columbia to check for regulatory and policy compliance. This effort is governed by Army Regulation 11-1 Command Logistics Review Program (CLRP).

During the state visits, I did an in-brief as deputy to the chief (at that time, it was Colonel Bruce Walton). I told the states (whether it was California or New Hampshire or Missouri or Indiana) the following: "You are running your state and it's open for business. And it's working." I would go on, "We are not here to tell you what to do, or how and when to conduct your business. Instead we are here only to check to see that what you are doing is in compliance with regulatory standards and policy—and furthermore to share best business practices and lessons learned—that we have had the opportunity to glean from other states that we have visited; and lastly, to assist you to be in compliance."

As you can imagine, whenever a team arrives from the national headquarters to conduct an inspection, it can cause a bit of consternation and stress, perceived or otherwise. I thought it was our role to set the stage for our (and their) success by outlining our approach—and the boss supported it.

With that, the tension in the room would quiet down. After that, we went about doing the Army's work. I trusted that they saw the passion I had for this branch and the work of the U.S. Armed Services.

JACO and Beyond

Following the CLRT assignment, I then went to serve as the Chief of the Executive Secretariat in the National Guard Joint Action Control Office (JACO) at The Pentagon. I was responsible for coordinating the collaboration of relevant stakeholders in all staff actions for the Chief of the National Guard.

My final assignment of my military career was to be the Counter Drug Commander for the New York City Region Counter Drug Taskforce. My responsibilities included planning, managing, coordinating, collaborating with, and supporting local, federal, and state law enforcement agencies. I did this by providing criminal and financial crimes analysts as well as community coalition teams to work with grassroots organizations in local New York city and state communities—to do everything from assisting them with grant writing for community projects, to assisting communities with efforts to meaningfully engage the youth. This was particularly crucial, especially during the opioid epidemic.

***

CHAPTER 5
Deployment and HaDR

"Travel is fatal to prejudice, bigotry and narrow-mindedness, and many of our people need it sorely on these accounts." –Mark Twain

While in the military, I was deployed to Tikrit in Iraq; Cairo and Alexandria in Egypt; Kuala Lumpur in Malaysia; Tegucigalpa and Jesus de Otoro in Honduras; and other parts of Latin America and various parts of Africa.

In these endeavors, my role was doing operations and logistics for whatever the mission was. I can assure you that movement into theatre is heavy logistics. You have everything from chicken and salad to tanks and aircraft. I had to decide on the capabilities and what to prioritize to meet the intent of the commander.

When I was on my way to Tikrit, Iraq, I wondered why they would call a Forward Operating Base "FOB Danger." It sounded so ominous. Why would they use the word "danger" in the description? But when I got there, I quickly realized why. The insurgents immediately greeted us with small arms fire and rockets!

Classes of Supply

A Supply Officer (NCO) is responsible for planning, coordinating, and delivering everything from "beans to bullets" in the Army. Logistics is interesting in that you're literally thinking through what someone or a group of persons will need; first for their sustainment, and then for the mission.

We use *classes* of supply as a guide to ensure that we hit all the proper functions. Class 1, for example, would be food, so all meals. I'll give an example: Jim Smith and John Doe are on a team and they're moving out on mission for a week. The supply officer, usually a sergeant, will sit and calculate in detail what they will need in terms of meals. One week is seven days, which at three meals a day makes 21 meals. For one week, each person must be supplied with three gallons of water, and so on. Supply officers really get down into the details.

Class 2 would be end items for office-type things: paper, markers, and pens. Class 3 would be fuel, bulk, retail, and oils for driving vehicles, flying helicopters or other aircraft. They need fuel, whether it's bulk or retail. And we'd calculate and resource those throughout the movement. Class 4 is construction and barrier materials. That's anything from plywood to concertina wiring, nails—all those things needed for construction, mobility, and counter-mobility. So the logistics person would sit down and calculate those and resource them.

Class 5 is ammunition, including everything from small arms to the big stuff like missiles. So, at the company level you're talking small potatoes, as we say: 9 mm, M4s and M16s, which are 5.56 mm rounds, machine guns with 50 caliber rounds, mortars, and rockets, and so on. So, we would research and resource. We'd pick up and we'd secure. As you can imagine, because we were dealing with ammunition, there were strict rules and regulations regarding safeguarding and handling of these items.

Class 6 is personal items like soap, deodorant, and alcohol. The military will provide some of them, but most soldiers have their own. Class 7 are major end items like trucks, aircraft, and artillery guns. If you think of major end items, war tanks are certainly among them. And depending on the organization, possibly bulldozers, scrapers, and all types of heavy equipment. Class 8 is all medical. When you're doing dangerous things, people are going to get hurt. They're going to get shot. So we have to make sure we have medical supplies on hand and qualified medical personnel to take care of them.

Class 9 is spare parts. Moving and firing weapons means that things will break and we'll need to fix them. Parts to fix them will also be sourced and provided for the mission.

Class 10 is off-the-shelf commercial items that one can go into Home Depot or Lowes or Sears to buy to use in support of work—things that the military will not supply, or does not have in its inventory, because it's not cost-effective for them to carry. Or you may be in an area where you can't get them, so it is easier just to take a credit card and go get them from the local hardware store and buy what you need. I'm referring to simple things, such as batteries. We'd go to Staples and buy them, as well as items like printers or printer cartridges.

So, I just went through what a Supply Officer or NCO uses as his or her guide to keep the soldiers and the organization and the mission resourced. Supply officers and NCOs really get down into the details.

I served in this capacity with love. If I didn't, it could've been disastrous.

Humanitarian Assistance Disaster Relief

I did some work with Humanitarian Assistance and Disaster Relief (HaDR). I had an assignment to go to the Middle East. I was also involved with HaDR planning and logistics in Central America. In Nicaragua, there was abject poverty. But we were always well received there.

Our mission was to help civilians in danger, whether it was civilians in the battlefield or civilians caught in a natural disaster such as a flood, famine or fire. In the U.S. National Guard, we have a responsibility to save these people.

Seven Hundred Pages

Military planning is a niche that I found I enjoy. I like the discipline of it. It includes keen attention to detail. If I have to examine the hair on a mosquito's ass, I will. A high level of detail is what I like. At one point, we even wrote a 700-page operations manual.

It's up to me to uncover every stone and communicate it to the boss. They need good information in order to make good decisions, whether it's civil affairs or psychological warfare.

I have experienced many instances where officers have undermined the boss. It didn't turn out well. In fact, it was very unproductive. I now realize that it has to be clearly understood that there is one boss. Dispense with all the nonsense and get to work.

The leaders I admired were about the Army. They were selfless. They weren't about the parochialisms and clannish other crap. Their only work was the Army. They were fair. Selflessness is key to leadership, which is why I think leadership is lacking in government, sports and entertainment, religion, business, and families.

In my 32 years in the military, there were only a handful of commanders that I really admired and respected. Maybe five or six. It's sad. In an organization that prides itself on leadership and discipline, that's terrible. Most of them were incompetent and selfish and totally forgot why they signed up to serve there. They certainly didn't demonstrate courage, integrity, passion, or love for one another.

***

CHAPTER 6
Benefits of the Army National Guard

"The true soldier fights not because he hates what is in front of him, but because he loves what is behind him."—G.K. Chesterton

We fight for the guy and gal on our left and on our right.

The military, for the most part, takes care of its veterans. And, fortunately, there is no longer a draft. If you serve for 20 years in the reserves, typically you will retire with about a $3,000-a-month pension for the rest of your life, starting at age 62. If you were an enlisted soldier or commissioned officer on active duty for those 20 years, you could essentially retire between 38 and 42 years of age and get a pension. How cool is that?

As I told soldiers I worked with, "Only in these great United States will this happen."

My greatest honor being an officer in the army came whenever recruiters knocked on my office door and asked me to perform the Oath of Enlistment for a young man or woman to join the military. I stopped everything I was doing to complete this function. I thought it was a tremendous privilege and it gave me great pleasure to tell a young person to raise their right hand to take the oath or to be retained in the army following the conclusion of their initial term of enlistment.

If I was in the middle of a meeting, I would pause and stop the meeting to complete this function. My most cherished moment of administering this oath was when I traveled to a Harrisburg, Pennsylvania recruiter's office and told my son Daniel to raise his right hand to take the oath when he joined the Pennsylvania Army National Guard. In a small way, I felt that I played a role and I was contributing to the recruitment, training, and replacement of the guardians at the gate for our great country.

Many of my leadership discussions with young men and women (and soldiers who were retained) went something like this: I started with the question, "How much do you think the government has paid to convert you from a civilian to a soldier? Take a guess." And then I would wait a little while for their response before answering.

"Try $90,000!"

That blows their mind. "Uncle Sam and the American people think you are worthy enough to take $90,000 plus—upfront—and spend it on you," I would go on. "Mind you, they haven't asked you to do anything yet. That's just based on your potential!

"Because that's what it takes to put you though basic training and AIT and set up a $400,000 life insurance policy to support your next of kin, including a $100,000 death gratuity for your spouse. Also, in addition to your medical benefits, you get dental and vision/optometry. Oh! And an M4 Carbine that you're going to be using is now assigned to you. They have just spent $4,000 to purchase that weapon for you. They'll also provide you with uniforms.

"Oh, and, by the way, it doesn't stop. That is just to get you to the entry-level training. Okay? What you have to do is you show up to this armory to work, and then the schooling starts.

"After the basic entry-level training, in two to three years, you get to go to the Warrior Leader Course. That is two weeks with a couple weeks preparation. Guess how much that costs?

"Another $16,000! For two weeks. Oh, and by the way, you get paid a full-time salary while you are doing it. Prorated.

"You complete that and you're still training and going to school, coming in doing your work part-time. Guess what the next school is after that?

"Your BLC: (Basic Leaders Course). Guess how much that costs?

"Try $18,000. Shout it out!

"This is all for your personal and professional development—to make you an American fighting hero! After that, you have ALC (Advanced Leaders Course). Guess how much that costs?

"$39,000! After ALC, you have your SLC (Senior Leader Course). Guess how much that costs?

"$42,000!

"If you survive all of this work, training, and schooling, and become eligible, you get to attend the top senior non-commissioned officers' school, the Sergeant Majors Academy. If you are an officer and you survive all of the required schooling, plus your special schools, and if you're eligible to take sabbatical leave, you can attend an Ivy League university like Harvard and earn a master's degree. All courtesy and fully paid for by your rich Uncle Sam and the American people.

"And after 20 years, you get a retirement—and the VA (Veterans Affairs) picks you up and tracks your medical, for life.

"Somebody lied to you. This is not a part-time job."

And then I ask them, "Do you know any part-time job that does this?" I conclude, "So understand the reason why I say there's a commitment that I need from you. And, as such, I need for you to start thinking about it a certain way—differently from the way you've been thinking about it. The National Guard is a career, not a part-time job."

If You Don't Come Back

There is always the inevitable question, "What if I don't come back?"

There is a two-phase process that takes place upon the death of a soldier. The first phase is the notification phase, and the second is the assistance phase. The entire process is treated with great reverence.

During phase one, a chaplain goes to the house of the family with a Casualty Notification Officer (CNO) to notify the next of kin about the death of his or her soldier and delivers a $100,000 death gratuity. That is to reduce the worry of the family, knowing that in many cases the soldier was the primary breadwinner in the house. It is to help lessen the burden. The family will still have to grieve. But they shouldn't have to worry about finances.

Following the notification, there's a Casualty Assistance Officer (CAO) who will provide support, guidance, and assistance to the next-of-kin of the soldier. They spend as much time as is necessary to help them throughout the entire grieving process. I have heard of instances where assistance officers have spent as much as six months with the family member. That family becomes the place of work for the CAO.

If a soldier perishes while on duty, the beneficiary gets a $400,000 life insurance policy within 30 days after the death. The attention paid to the individual soldier is unparalleled.

America is not just any country and it is itself a fighting force that I don't think the world has ever seen. From the beginning of time, there have been other countries with large forces—countries like China, India, and Korea. But the benefits previously mentioned make us different.

The United States Takes its Military Very Seriously

When young men and women are considering joining the National Guard, I often tell them, "The U.S. military budget exceeds the combined GDP of all countries in Africa." I say that and they just chuckle.

But just chew on that for a minute. Africa encompasses an entire continent—800 million people. Let's say 500 million of them work. It's an impressive number, when you think about it! That's why we can afford to pay more than a trillion dollars for one aircraft-related program. Or, more than $7,000,000 for a tank! This is a bit of an exaggeration, but it's not far from the truth.

The Need for the Guard

Serving in the military is a form of leadership. But there needs to be leaders within the military to make it run properly. Readiness, as far as the National Guard is concerned, can easily mean the difference between life and death for those in the community.

Today the National Guard averages about 20,000 soldiers and airmen mobilized in places like Afghanistan, Syria, Iraq, the Sinai, Europe, and South America. At home, locally the National Guard deals with hurricanes, floods, earthquakes, wildfires, tornadoes, and other natural disasters.

The Army National Guard comprises over one third of the Army's manpower and provides nearly 40 percent of the Army's operational force. The branch has supported over 850,000 overseas deployments.

The (National Guard) Bureau

The National Guard Bureau is the federal instrument that was created by the Militia Act of 1903. It's a joint bureau of the Department of the Army and the Department of the Air Force. The National Defense Authorization Act for Fiscal Year 2008 elevated the National Guard to a joint function of the Department of Defense.

This act also elevated the rank of the Chief of the National Guard Bureau (CNGB) from three stars to four when Craig R. McKinley, United States Air Force, took the helm. The Bureau holds a unique status as both a staff and command operations agency.

As I write this, the Chief of the National Guard Bureau is Gen. Joseph L. Lengyel. I served under Frank J. Grass, followed by Gen. Lengyel, as their Chief Executive Secretariat. It was an honor and a privilege because of opportunities to be present, and to listen, watch, and learn decision-making and leading.

The National Guard Bureau has three core missions: fighting to win America's wars, securing the homeland, and building enduring partnerships around the world.

***

PART 2

CLIP

Christians believe that God sends the Holy Spirit to dwell within us, giving us energy, intelligence, imagination, and love to be Christ's faithful disciples in the world. Similarly, I believe that there are four pillars of leadership. I submit to you that they are courage, love, integrity, and passion.

The acronym is CLIP—and I can assure you it beats the hell out of PTSD! Courage, love, integrity, and passion are, for me, "check the box" criteria items that, when demonstrated, prompt others to look at you and say, "That's a leader." If CLIP was a fabric, people would be the common thread that is interwoven throughout the fabric. As a result, if you were to remove one component of the fabric, you destroy that fabric and change its structure, meaning, and existence. All components of CLIP are directly related to people.

But here's a secret! We each have the ability to bring these things to bear on just about anything. Ergo, everyone has inherent leadership abilities.

Overview

I will touch briefly on each CLIP component before we get into more depth in subsequent chapters.

Simon Sinek says that "*Courage* is an external thing." He insists that the reason people throw themselves into harm's way or put their lives on the line for someone else is because others would do the same for them. This is the reason why someone who displays real courage would violate all tenets of survival to save another life, he insists.

When I think of *love*, I think foremost of Jesus Christ. He paid the ultimate price—for all mankind. Next, I think of Gandhi, who said, "Where there is love, there is life." And, last but certainly not least, Reverend Dr. Martin Luther King, Jr., is a more contemporary example. These three leaders, in my opinion, embodied the essence of the four pillars of leadership—courage, love, integrity, and passion.

For *integrity,* you could easily substitute the word "trust," which is also synonymous with "honesty." It is important to have integrity in all aspects of your life when dealing with other people, and it begins with yourself. Treat yourself with integrity first.

And finally, if I can inspire just one person to follow a *passion* that they've identified, then I will have succeeded. I'm not going to say I can find it for you, because that's on you. But if you have identified a passion within you for something you didn't think about or pay attention to before reading this book, then a lightbulb has come on. It is all about your passion, stupid!

CHAPTER 7
Courage

"A ship is safe in harbor, but that's not what ships are built for."
—John A. Shedd

I believe that the first pillar of leadership is courage. Courage is defined as "the ability to do something that frightens one." Put another way, it is "strength in the face of pain or grief." Regardless of which definition you subscribe to, the reality is there is always an element of fear involved. Stated another way, for me the rock band The Script succinctly captured courage in the lyrics to their song, "Superheroes" when they wrote, "That's how a superhero learns to fly every day, every hour, turn the pain into power."

I have often been one to "feel the fear but do it anyway." Now I realize that fear isn't such a bad thing. In fact, in some translations of the Bible, such as the New International Version, the word "fear" is sometimes replaced with "reverence."

Perhaps you are aware that "fear not" is the most repeated command in the Bible. In fact, I have heard that there are 365 "fear nots" in the Bible—one "fear not" for every day of the year! I have also heard that Lloyd Ogilvie, in *Facing the Future without Fear,* said there are 366, including one for Leap Year! A person without the component of courage will not experience living. Life is tough and you need courage to engage in it daily.

Derivation

The root of the word courage is cor—the Latin word for heart. Brené Brown says, "Courage starts with showing up and letting ourselves be seen." She goes on to say, "Truth and courage aren't always comfortable, but they're never weakness."

Courage to step out is a very admirable trait. To the person displaying it, it often results in a point where you're all alone. "I'm the one," you think to yourself. Most people will not do something if they feel they're out there by themselves. Those people say, "Misery loves company." They like to be in a group.

That is because at that moment their passion has not been ignited. On the other hand, you'll find few people who welcome it because their passion was ignited. It was their time. They don't even think about it. "I'm going to step up and step out," they might say, or, "If it's to be, it's up to me." It takes courage to do so. Stepping out of that comfort zone makes you vulnerable. You often realize the moment of truth when you are the only one standing there doing it.

Getting Out of Your Comfort Zone

Courage comes in many shapes and sizes—as well as in a variety of situations. What's your comfort zone? Displaying courage could be something as simple as teeing off in front of a group of people on a golf course. To the Tiananmen Square Tank Man, it was defiantly blocking the path of a column of tanks heading east on Beijing's Chang'an Boulevard on June 5, 1989.

My point is no other person could have done what the lone Chinese man did, from the beginning of time to the present and into the future. There will never ever be another Chinese tank man. What he accomplished was unique to him and no one else. Like Dr. Martin Luther King, Jr., Gandhi, and Jesus Christ, their action (or lack of a reaction) perhaps cost them their lives. But, as Dr. King said, "It doesn't matter anymore." It takes a strong demonstration of love to arrive at that point in your passion to lead. Great leaders are lovers and great leaders treat themselves with integrity before demonstrating integrity with others.

So, if you're motivated to get out there and do it—but, if you're reticent and you're holding back, not wanting to make a mistake—I say, "Nonsense!"

Why do you fear stepping out and making a mistake? Why not concern yourself with doing what needs to be done well? You know, if you're going to make a mistake, it's going to happen. You're not going to be able to stop it. Instead, let me invite you to think about it this way: There is no mistake because it is your passion. No one can judge your mistake but you. No one knows the benchmark and metrics for the success of your passion but you. So, the only person to see and know your mistake is you.

Concentrate on doing well the action inspired by your courage. Because, by default, you're going to make mistakes as defined by you. You are human. And if you are going to make a mistake, it's okay! The word mistake is only a label. Change the label and call it something else, as long as you don't get anybody killed and you're not destroying anybody's property or life or limb. And oh, by the way, it's probably something you learn from tremendously. The focus on doing it and having the courage to do it with love and integrity allows your passion.

I submit to you that we all have that. That's why I make the statement that leadership traits reside in each of us. We all have the ability to be that leader. And my hope is when you decide to spend your money to buy this book (if you haven't done so already) and then spend the time reading it (which you're obviously doing now), that you'll pick out some tools—and that you'll store these concepts in your leadership tool bag that you carry with you at all times. And you'll thereby inspire the leader that's in you, for whatever the cause.

Martin Treptow

When I think of courage, I often think of Martin Treptow. Treptow left his job as a small-town barber in 1917 to go to France. He had enlisted in the Iowa National Guard, which became the 168th Infantry Regiment, 84th Brigade, in the 42nd "Rainbow" Division, when it was called to Federal service. Private Treptow was killed while serving as a runner, or courier, for Company M in July of 1918.

After he was killed, a diary was found on him that included this pledge: "America must win this war. Therefore, I will work, I will save, I will sacrifice, I will endure, I will fight cheerfully and do my utmost, as if the issue of the whole struggle depended on me alone."

President Ronald Reagan alluded to Treptow in his first inaugural address to the nation. If you watch the footage of Reagan delivering the speech, you'll see that even he gets choked up when he's recollecting the story.

A Message to Garcia

Another example that inspires me is, "A Message to Garcia." You may be familiar with it. The gist of it is when there's a task to be done, it has to be done. And effective leaders want to get things done. It's *do*, not *ask*: over the top, into the breach, and accomplish the mission.

The legend goes that during the Spanish American war, President William McKinley gave Lieutenant Andrew S. Rowan a letter to be delivered to General Calixto Garcia, a leader of the Cuban insurgents, somewhere in the mountain vastness of Cuba (no one knew where) asking him to do something. Rowan did not ask where Garcia was or how he should go about getting it to him, yet he succeeded. The bottom line was, and is, to get it done.

A silent movie entitled A Message to Garcia was made about Rowan's mission in 1916 by Thomas Edison. In 1936, 20th Century Fox made a "talkie" about Rowan. The story is about loyalty. Most people are unwilling to stay on task. It exemplifies individual initiative and conscientiousness in work.

After 31 years in the military, I have concluded that there are two roles in the army—or any other organization in this world for that matter. One is when you're doing command time or you're in charge and the other is when you're doing staff time or are a team member supporting those who are in charge. Very few of us get the opportunity to be commanders. I was fortunate enough to be in both roles on numerous occasions—and I submit to you that we all become fortunate enough to fill both roles at some time or another in our lives.

As a staff person or team member, you have one answer and it begins and ends with "Yes." Some people object to this philosophy. The rule, however, is that as long as what the commanding officer or the person in charge is asking you to do is not immoral or illegal, it must be done. The operating words are immoral or illegal. My role as a commander, and the role of anyone in charge, is to make decisions. And the role of the supporting staff or team members is to execute that decision if it does not violate legal and moral boundaries. While this is a simplistic explanation, it is the BLUF—or bottom-line up front. The back story, of course, is that as support staff, we identify relevant stakeholders, collaborate, coordinate, and negotiate, as well as solicit input and feedback to arrive at a product that we present to the decision maker for a verdict. Oftentimes you will have to redo or be asked to synthesize two or more ideas to get a final decision, but generally that's how we work.

Acquiescence is hard for many soldiers and civilian team members to swallow. But the reality is, when they're in a command position, they see how important it is. If everyone agreed to this doctrine, things would run a lot smoother.

We All Want Solutions

I am reminded of a slogan that says, in Spanish, "No presente problemas. Soluciones!" In other words, "Don't present problems. Give me solutions!"

At any particular moment, you might need courage to approach a decision maker. You could rationalize not doing so by telling yourself, "Most people get shot down, so I'm not even going to bother." But usually you don't know until you try, and if you do get shot down, rise back up, regroup, and re-engage. Courage, like leadership itself, is a trait that is in every one of us.

Most people, by nature, are kind of shy. I do concede that there are those who are brash and think the world revolves around them. But they're usually the exception. Leaders, and people with courage, are not always the people you think they are. They are ordinary people who do extraordinary things when their passions are ignited.

The bottom line is no one is willing to die for a cause that is not their passion. But if it is their passion, courage elevates them from the crowd, allowing them to step out. Love allows them to reconcile integrity within themselves and others, and passion fuels their possibilities. These are some of the reasons why I believe courage is the first of the Four Pillars of Leadership.

***

CHAPTER 8
Love

"The best and most beautiful things in this world cannot be seen or even heard, but must be felt with the heart."—Helen Keller

Niccolò Machiavelli, with respect to leadership, said, "It is better to be feared than loved." Well, with all due respect, Niccolò, you did not know people like I have come to know people. Even though your reference was about your clients, who were the elite and powerful rulers of your time, when you lead with love, you don't only elevate the human spirit and open a deep well of creativity and innovative ideas, you discover that people love you in return because of the way you treat them.

As a team leader, you will find that you have to tap on the desks of your followers to tell them to go home long past the workday, and when they get home, they can't wait to return the following morning.

I often say that I'm in love with this girl called Army. A story is told that General Colin Powell's wife made a statement once at a party after he retired. "There was always another woman in our relationship," she said. There was a gasp in the room and everybody was thinking, "What is she talking about?" She went on, "She's always been there and I knew about her and I was okay with her... this girl named 'Army.' She was unrelenting. She kept weird hours. She would call all the time. And he'd always have to respond." People who didn't understand General Powell's commitment beforehand, now did.

You think it was the army, but in reality it was her husband, the General, reacting and living in the place he had discovered where he could express unending agape love for his soldiers. He was never tired because it was not work. You can replace the army with any organization or cause in this world and you will find the equivalent of General Powell in both male and female leaders.

Leaders are Lovers

Effective leaders are in love with what they do. You have to be in love with what you do to derive a passion for it—otherwise you're not going to spend the inordinate amount of time required to do it well and achieve success.

Love also comes into play with the people side of things. I think most of us can see the parallel between love and people. Passion is more about things. Managing is more about things. I can like the redwoods. I can manage a construction project. I can like cars. I can manage a fleet of trucks or cars and I can be passionate about auto racing.

But I can't speak the same way about people. When it comes to people, you have to lead and not manage them. In order to effectively lead people, you have to love people. There are those who would argue and say, "Well, it is just a play on words." But I think speaking and hearing about love resonates internally with a person. It makes you feel differently.

The people are what is important—and in my mind leadership equates to people only. Although it may sound counterintuitive, for example, you cannot lead a construction project and you cannot lead a fleet of trucks or cars.

That's why I say that leaders are lovers. Leaders love people. You cannot effectively lead without love.

Empathy

You demonstrate leadership to people because that's what they need. For example, let's say it is 0700 hours, and you're getting ready to go to your morning staff meeting. A member of your team calls and says, "Hey I'm going to be late," or "I can't come in today because I didn't get any sleep. My 9-month-old was up all night with a fever and we just got back home from the emergency room at 6:30 this morning."

What does a **leader** do when they get that information—versus what does a **manager** do when they get that information? My expectation is that a leader looks around, calls out to a team member and says, "Hey Mark, Steve just called. He can't come in. He's been up all night with Adrian. I need you to step in the gap and cover the key items today. Can you do that?"

At that point, that's all Mark needs to know. And Mark would probably say yes, if the leader has created the right culture on that team. Because anyone else on the squad could have had a problem. It took 10 seconds of your time to find a solution instead of overreacting ("Oh my God! You're out again! The world is going to come to an end!"). That's not what Steve needs to hear. He's telling you that his child was in the hospital and they didn't get home until 6:30 this morning!

Of course, we can embark on or use the style that you see most leaders use: intimidation, humiliation, and fear. I think that comes from a lack of good mentors, good experience, or a good background. In West Africa where I come from, we say that you were "unbrought-up." Leading from the standpoint of intimidation, humiliation, and fear is not the preferred method and does not work.

Love as a Pillar of Leadership?

Some might say, "I've got courage. I've got integrity and passion. But love?" Yes, agape love, the love of strangers or people. This is love that was demonstrated by all great and successful leaders like Christ, Gandhi, Mother Teresa, and Martin Luther King, Jr., just to name a few.

I think we downplay love or marginalize it because it isn't cool. We think it deals with religion, and our society says, "Don't touch that!" But when a person leads with love, it is felt and experienced by all the people on the team. They focus not only on their performance and potential, but she concentrates on how to leverage their strengths against the weaknesses of the other team members. She studies what motivates them to elevate them to their next level of achieving.

Love really does heal. It is why diversity works. I have noticed that whenever we've combined black and white on our teams, we have experienced some of the most amazing results we've ever seen. In my training, I use the analogy of the keyboard. You've got black keys and you have white keys. Try playing a keyboard and saying to yourself, "I'm only going to use the black keys." Let me know how that worked out for you and see how your music sounds. Or, "I'm only going to use the white keys." See how your music sounds. I'll bet it doesn't sound the same as when you decide to use all the keys.

While a basic foundation for teaching early childhood education is ordering and differentiating things, effective leaders know that this does not apply to people. Instead you need to mix people up and leverage their strengths.

We are especially adept at marginalizing women—due to falsehoods, misconceptions, and stupid practices that we learned as children, taught to us by the adults around us. Collectively, we are all smaller in every way because we left out and did not consider the female perspective.

It reminds me of the movie that came out a few years ago entitled *Hidden Figures*. It was about a team of black women that did work for NASA behind the scenes. I use it as an example when I talk about what women bring to the table. These women were able to do calculations on the order of minutes, whereas it might've taken others hours, or days. There was a leader who realized that these women were onto something.

We marginalize women, the handicapped, and all different kinds of people because of incompetence and fear—and our corporations and countries, as well as the people we attempt to lead, suffer immensely for it.

And yet, every instance where leaders include different kinds of people in work situations endeavoring to derive solutions, the results have been phenomenal! And so, I never understood why it is that we keep circling back to where we're always at each other's throats: isolating, separating, and dividing, based on differences. What is wrong with people?!

The African Continent

Look at the African continent. We have people who are white and they're Africans. You have people who are dark and they are Africans, too! The continent is the one place on this earth where diverse populations, ethnic groups, all sizes and shapes of people converge in one place. And yet, unlike the black and white keys on a keyboard, leaders have not learned how to leverage the strengths of each for the good of the community, or the continent-at-large. In theory it should be the best of places to live and experience life because of its vast and different peoples, cultures, and traditions. Effective leaders who lead with love recognize that there is power and strength in differences and not necessarily in sameness. Remember that where two of us agree on everything, then one of us becomes unnecessary.

The African continent has two deserts. You have the Sahara up north. It's huge. It is larger than the size of the United States, about one and a quarter times the size of the U.S. Then you go all the way through the continent and down toward South Africa to the Kalahari Desert and Namib Desert near the West Coast.

The population of Bushmen who live there are small people. They are on average less than 5 feet tall. If you go to Tanzania, Burundi, and Uganda you have people who are 7 feet to 8 feet tall. If you go to northern Tanzania and central and southern Kenya, you will meet the Maasai people, whose average height is also 6 to 7 feet tall. They're all Africans! I say, "If you want to see God's demonstration and love for variety and differences, look at the African continent!"

God loves variety. He has a sense of humor, too. He truly does.

Love is on the Move

Unlike courage, integrity, and passion, without love, nothing happens. In the military, the transporters always say that nothing happens until something moves. Nothing could be truer. Love is what distinguishes a good leader from a great leader. Leadership is getting people to do what you want them to do. Simply stated, you cannot get people to do what you want them to do because of who you are. Instead, you will get people to do what you want them to do because of the way you make them feel.

I learned a concept early in my officer career, as a newly commissioned second lieutenant, that "soldiers don't care how much you know until they know how much you care." A leader caring about the team and the people is a demonstration of love. Love permeates the fabric that is called leadership. It is interwoven throughout to hold courage, integrity, and passion in place in the fabric.

Every good team leader wants an engaged team that is made up of engaged individuals. That is because engaged team members are self-motivated. I submit that this is not a forgone conclusion. Instead, leading with love is the spark that ignites this phenomenon in your team members. This is important because when leaders inspire and empower the people they lead, teams and members become elevated to that next level, resulting in creativity and innovation.

Leading people with love is a continuous process improvement for leadership. Effective leaders always reflect on the fact that there is always room for self-improvement. To effectively succeed as a leader, you have to be dynamic and not static, to be flexible and not rigid, to be understanding and open to what the people you are leading are telling you, without being cold and aloof to their plight, waiting for them to fumble and humiliate themselves.

To lead with love is the direct opposite of being feared as a leader. In revisiting Machiavelli's quote at the opening of this chapter, that it is better to be feared than loved (because fear is stronger than being liked or loved), this is the same mental-midget mindset that marginalized women because they were seen as weak. This is Cro-Magnon man mentality, and oh boy, were they wrong! I submit to any leader that subscribes to this notion that you are being placated if you think that the people you are leading love you. The people you lead don't love you. Instead they hate you and they will seek every opportunity to undermine all of your efforts at getting anything done.

Parallel Lives

To make my point about the effectiveness of leading with love by using as examples some famous people such as Jesus, Gandhi, Martin Luther King, Jr., and Mother Teresa, I will contrast them with some of the most feared and ruthless leaders of all time. A popular maxim says, "One man's hero is another man's tyrant." Attila the Hun (AD 434-453), after killing his brother to become the leader of the Hunnic Empire, centered in present day Hungary, expanded the empire to present-day Germany, Russia, Ukraine, and the Balkans. "There, where I have passed, the grass will never grow gain," he remarked on his reign. Genghis Khan (1206-1227) spent time as a slave during his teenage years before he united the Mongol tribes and went on to conquer a huge part of Central Asia and China. He was characterized as brutal, and historians noted that he slaughtered civilians en masse.

Timur, who reigned from 1370-1405, really relished being feared. He led military campaigns through a large part of western Asia, including modern Iran and Syria.

In present-day Afghanistan, he ordered the construction of a tower made out of living men, one stacked on top of another and cemented together. He also ordered a massacre to punish a rebellion and had 70,000 heads built up into minarets.

Queen Mary I (1553-1558), aka Bloody Mary, was the only child of King Henry VIII and Catherine of Aragon. Mary I became queen of England in 1553 and soon reinstalled Catholicism (after previous rulers championed Protestantism) as the main religion—and married Philip II of Spain, a Catholic. Over the next few years, hundreds of Protestants were burned at the stake. After that, she earned the nickname "Bloody Mary."

Not to be outdone, and obviously not students of the history that preceded them, the following list of modern leaders continued with the notion that it is better to be feared than to be loved as a leader:

- Vladimir Lenin (1917-1924) led the October Revolution to overturn the provisional government that had overthrown the Czar. During this period of revolution, war and famine, Lenin demonstrated a chilling disregard for the sufferings of his fellow countrymen and mercilessly crushed any opposition.
- Following Lenin, Joseph Stalin (1922-1953), forced quick industrialization and collectivization in the 1930s that coincided with mass starvation, the imprisonment of people in labor camps, and the Great Purge of the intelligentsia, the government and the armed forces. He killed over 20 million of his countrymen.
- Who can forget Germany's Adolf Hitler, who reigned from 1933-1945? By the end of 1941, his Third Reich empire (and Axis) included almost every country in Europe plus a large part of North Africa. He devised a plan to create his ideal "master race" by eliminating Slavs, gypsies, homosexuals, Jews, and other political opponents by forcefully sending them into concentration camps, where they were tortured to death. According to reports, the Nazis killed about 11 million people under Hitler's regime.

- In Asia, during the 1949-1976 reign of communist leader Mao Zedong, industry and agriculture was put under state control in China. Any opposition was swiftly suppressed. Mao's supporters point out that he modernized China. Others point out that his policies led to the deaths of 40 million people through starvation, forced labor and executions.
- Over on the African continent, Idi Amin overthrew an elected government in Uganda via a military coup and declared himself president (1971-1979). He then ruthlessly ruled for eight years, during which an estimated 3 million civilians were massacred. He also drove out Uganda's Asian-African population (mostly Indian-African and Pakistani-African citizens), and spent large amounts on the military, both of which led to the country's economic decline.
- In South America, Chile's Augusto Pinochet, in power from 1973 until 1990, overthrew Chile's government with the help of a U.S.-backed coup. Reports say numerous people "disappeared" under the regime and 35,000 were tortured. Pinochet died before he could stand trial on accusations of human-rights abuses.

A New Way of Leading

The recognition and incorporating of love in the leadership paradigm is a relatively new and post-1980 phenomenon. As technology continues to develop at an accelerated pace, the way we work is changing quickly and differently. Globalization implies that the people we collaborate with are often sitting at the other end of the world, speaking different languages and living in another culture, making human interaction more fragile.

We don't leave our humanness at home when we go to work and we want to know that our team members respect us, recognize us, and care for us. Most importantly, we want to be assured that the people who lead us do the same.

Jack Ma, founder and former executive chairman of Chinese multinational corporation Alibaba Group, reiterated at the World Economic Forum in Davos, Switzerland that leaders need IQ, EQ, and LQ—

the quotient of love. Ma went on to say, "A machine does not have a heart, a machine does not have a soul, and a machine does not have a belief. Human beings have souls, have the belief, and have the value; and only we have the ability to be creative."

Love is the Answer

Benjamin Franklin said, "If we do not hang together, we will most assuredly hang separately." So I ask, "Where is the fun in that?" As a leader, practice leading with love, and you will never work as hard as before in your team. I promise you. Try it.

***

CHAPTER 9
Integrity

"In looking for people to hire, look for three qualities: integrity, intelligence, and energy. And if they don't have the first, the other two ***will kill you.****" —Warren Buffett*

Leadership is having people do what you want them to do. In order to stand in front of a team or group and tell them, "I want you to do this," you need to be credible—and you will be credible only if you have integrity. They will listen to you if you have integrity. That's why integrity is one of those key elements that, for me, a leader must have.

When Cultures Collide

I don't tell this story lightly. Rather, I tell it in all humility.

It was January 2005, during Operation Iraqi Freedom 3 in Forward Operating Base (FOB) Danger, when I was in Tikrit, Iraq. Many of us had several jobs on the Division staff and one of mine was the Resource Manager for the Division's Iraqi Security Forces (ISF) Cell. The focus at that time was to prepare and assist in safeguarding the first-ever open and free Iraqi elections that were scheduled for January 30, 2005. And the way to do that was to put an Iraqi face on everything upfront, while the coalition presence had to become secondary and in the back. This was important in the worldview and in the presence of the local Iraqis.

The coalition forces would be in the background to respond in support of ISF, as needed, either at polling stations or in neighborhoods. This meant that Iraqi forces—Iraqi Soldiers (IS), Iraqi Police (IP), Department of Border Enforcement (DBE), Provincial Joint Coordination Centers (PJCC), Joint Coalition Centers (JCC), and Force Protection Services (FPS)—had to dress for success with uniform, weapons, and personal protective ballistic gear. The coalition forces closed down the border several days prior to the start of elections, to mitigate a surge in insurgent activities to foil the elections.

As always, there are second- and third-order effects to every action that we take. And, for me, this meant that I could not get my delivery of critical equipment for the ISF just days before the first major elections in the country. The "So what?" was that POTUS had announced to the world that the Iraqis would be seen and would be in charge of their elections—not the coalition forces.

The day started as usual between 0430 and 0500 with a phone call on my secured army Voice Over Internet Provider (VOIP) phone. It was my contractor calling with an emergency to say that he could not enter Iraq from Syria. I informed him that the coalition forces had closed all of the border crossings from Iran, Turkey, Syria, Jordan, and Saudi Arabia.

At this time, he replied that he had rented a retrofitted Russian boxcar aircraft and was flying the equipment to Iraq, but that he needed a place to land safely. I reminded him that there was a war going on and that he would be shot down. He became frantic and worried—I could hear it in his voice.

After much running between my office on the third level and the first level of Saddam Hussein Palace in Tikrit, and coordinating with Robert Vicci, my buddy in G3 air operations, on authenticating the aircraft, my contractor was allowed to land at Forward Operating Base Speicher. During the offloading I was called every expletive known to man and every other name but a child of God. You see, nothing was palletized and there was no order as to how the boxes had been loaded onto the aircraft.

To understand what happened, you have to understand and appreciate the art of logistics. This was the complete opposite of that. Then, following coordination with Rich Harding and my other logistician buddies ("loggies" for short), to inventory and initiate distribution of the equipment, Rich put the contractor on a Blackhawk flight to Danger to link with me for payment—all of which was unplanned and unexpected.

I totally had to reprioritize the entire day and week with one phone call. When the contractor arrived, I was put in a situation where I was releasing $2.7 million American taxpayer dollars to a guy who was a contractor for just this one purchase. That's tremendous responsibility! And it's one that I took on proudly, and recognized the importance of what I was doing.

I had never seen $2.7 million dollars in my life—let alone handle it. But at the "CAGE" where we dispensed cash payments, due to the lack of a banking system in the country, my contractor had to find places to stash his $2.7 million dollars. Places I will refrain from mentioning here.

But when this man got the money, a bunch of things happened. He could not go out of the front gate because the intel people had informed us that from a considerable distance, the insurgents had their people taking pictures of everyone—mostly third country nationals (TCNs)—who did business with the Americans and the coalition. They took their photos and either tracked them down or killed their families.

And the contractor also knew that. So it wasn't safe for him to exit and enter through our front (main entrance) gates. These insurgents would sit across the street or far off and use binoculars to track him.

So I had to fly him to Baghdad out of Tikrit. I took him all the way to the helicopter pad where the helicopter operations were taking place. As we drove in my HMMWV, he flipped through one of the chunks of money like this, "Rrrrrrrr," took a stack, pulled it out and said, "That's yours."

I said, "Whoa, what are you doing?"

He announced, "It's yours."

I said, "No, I cannot accept it."

He insisted, "But this is the way we do business in the Middle East. It's expected. This is for you."

And I repeated, "No, I cannot accept it! I'm an American army officer. I get paid very well to do my job so I cannot accept another payment."

And he stated, "But when this unit came through, I gave Captain So-and-So money and I gave Lieutenant…"

And I declared, "Stop! I don't want to know any names!" I stuck my fingers in my ears and started saying, "Peanut butter, peanut butter, peanut butter." He must have thought that this was strange behavior, but I did not care. Americans are known to do much stranger things than this!

I then proclaimed, "Timeout! If you insist, I will make sure that we add your name to the blacklist and the Americans and coalition will not do any further business with you, ever. In other words, we will not request supplies through you and pay you."

He had a DoD ID to move freely in and out of the theater so I knew that he had been vetted through the highest levels. He blamed my attitude on the fact that I didn't understand the culture, and therefore he felt less confident.

But we have our rules in the United States. You don't accept money—and if you do, it can only be so much ($10, or whatever that amount is).

Wisdom is Greater Than Riches

I couldn't help but think, "What does a young, inexperienced, and impulsive 22-year-old man or woman do when faced with a bribe?" Because certainly, no one ever prepared me for it. And I was much older (43 years old at the time). I was caught off guard by the bribe, and it took some serious talking to this man to let him understand that this was unacceptable.

So we ended up settling. Because they have to give you something you must accept. And I said, "Okay, bring us some hors d'oeuvres or those baklava (little candy treats they make). Bring us two or three of those for the entire office and it will be very much appreciated." And he thought that was okay and I could see that he felt better. But that's their culture.

From the locals, we learned some things about the culture and we learned a few words. They told us about things like, "Don't show the bottom of your feet," and what the implications were. "Don't address women directly. It's not welcomed." We got those things. But some of the things we just never got. And I couldn't help but think that we didn't prepare our very young officers, the second lieutenants, first lieutenants, maybe some captains and the non-commissioned officers (NCOs) for some of those things. Leadership is a quality you can always use more of. So that's something I wish would be prevalent.

And then I need to work to see how to have more of that conversation because more and more, these are the kinds of fights that our military is going to be engaged in—small engagements with locally managed budgets, etc. You're not going to have big armies like you had in World War II in Europe where this fifth army is moving across and advancing to here or there.

Instead, we'll have small engagements, close quarters, in cities and towns where there are lots of civilians on the battlefield with many opportunities to purchase commercial, off-the-shelf equipment and supplies. When the country does not have a banking system (as will be the case most of the time during a war), everything purchased will have to be in cash, and, most likely it will be in U.S. dollars.

Your Soldiers Believe What They See

Obviously, it would have been easy to have taken the money. But I don't know that I would have been able to sleep at night. I have too much to consider. I was married, had two children, a mortgage, family and friends who respected me a great deal.

It was just too expensive a proposition and one that I felt I could never recover from. The best way to win some games is to never play them. However, the most important thing of all was this: my Specialist-E4 was the one driving my HMMWV on the way to the helicopter operations on that day. I had to make sure that he knew where I, as his officer, stood when it came to paybacks or kickbacks. First, this was against our United States laws. Second, it was wrong.

I remembered the teaching from one of my instructors in my Captains Career Course (CCC) at Fort Lee, VA, who said, "Your credibility with soldiers and the trust it engenders grows from their perception of your professional competence and personal ethics. Soldiers hear what you tell them but they believe what they see."

He went on to explain that, "If you correct a soldier for uniform violation, your uniform must be right. If you admonish a soldier for poorly maintained boots, then yours must be good—and today should not be the first time you cleaned yours.

"If you want to effectively encourage a soldier to try harder on the Physical Training test, to hang tough and squeeze out those last two push-ups, that soldier can never see you quit with time remaining in your two minutes—no matter what your score is."

I will never forget his closing. He said, "Everything in life is a graded event." And I understood that to mean that I should always seek to pass and not fail. Field Marshal Bernard L. Montgomery stated it best when he said, "The first thing a young officer must do when he joins the Army is to fight a battle, and that battle is for the hearts of his men. If he wins that battle and subsequent similar ones, his men will follow him anywhere; if he loses it, he will never do any real good."

The word "integrity" is derived from the root, "integer." You may remember that word from your high school math class. It means "a whole number." It's important to be a whole number, even more so in this day and age. To me, it is a matter of doing the right thing, even—and especially—if no one is watching.

***

CHAPTER 10
Passion

"Chase your passion, not your pension." —Denis Waitley

What stokes your furnace? What drives you? What are you passionate about?

Politics? Religion? The Environment? Women's issues? Civil rights? Arts? Find out whatever it is that drives you and engage in it. I guarantee that you will feel fulfilled and be able to make a decent living from doing it. You will elicit the "Wow" factor from people when you do it.

You'll know once you hit your passion. Because there will be two things you'll experience: timelessness and effortlessness.

It won't even be considered work because you will lose track of time when you're thinking about it and when you are doing it. Whenever you lose track of time and energy when you are engaged in doing something, that's when you know that you're doing something you have an affinity for.

Your creativity flows, unabated, helping to inspire the leader that is inside of you. Look for these things. Find that passion.

What's Your Purpose?

To begin the process of living a life of passion, ask yourself: What is my purpose? The problem is that many of us don't ask ourselves what we like and what we want to do with our lives. Asking the question triggers us to begin the search and the journey. Instead, we follow the abnormal way, which is to go to school, get a job, go shopping, and accumulate stuff. And we think that we are living. If you think that is living, wait until you discover your passion!

I noted that it is abnormal because it is living life and functioning in what I call the "default mode." Now when you purchase a new computer or cell phone, it comes with a default mode setting that was set at the factory. The factory settings were put in just to get you started. It is not meant for you to experience the full range of your device or instrument. To get that unique experience, you need to go into the advance setting mode. In the advance setting, you will personalize and internalize your experiences for that device and instrument.

The same holds true for your life. In the "advance setting" mode is where you will begin to live and it is the birthplace of passion. It is where you thrive. You will become your toughest critic and uncompromising to yourself. You will become unapologetic and self-driven and you will begin to search for others to enlist in your journey and experience.

You will recognize mediocrity and become intolerant with it in yourself and in others because you see every person for the potential that they have. Once you begin to spend the time thinking—and dreaming—about your passion constantly, you know you have found it. When you're talking to your friends, you're discussing it. When you're reading a book, you're thinking about it. You might not even realize it.

The passion begins to drive your performance. At the army combat simulations center there was a passion for high performance which drove us and we bought into it. It stated that high performance is an attitude, a philosophy and a way of life. It was all about the first-person singular pronoun, "I," and no one else. It accepted that the future can be created by your will and your work.

It recognized that thoughts create emotions—giving you the power to develop how you feel, how you respond, and how you empower those around you. High performance is excelling to excel again. To paraphrase Theodore Roosevelt, it is better to dare mighty things, to win glorious triumphs, even though checkered with failure, than to rank with those poor spirits who neither enjoy much nor suffer much because they live in the grey twilight that knows not victory nor defeat.

High performance accepts that I must change if I am to grow. If I do not grow, what good am I to myself or anyone else? If change is the key to life, desire is the key to change. We must never give up or compromise our desire to live our lives to the fullest extent that God permits. This is the meaning of living your life in the advance setting mode instead of the default setting. Passion, like life, is a gift. Life is God's gift to you. Passion is your gift to yourself.

Once you've identified your purpose, you'll find that you've struck a chord. You've made a connection. Then, the next thing you should do—and not forget—is to take a step in that direction. Take that thought and energy and translate it into some kind of action. Even if it's in a very small way. It might be a cause: social, political, religious, entertainment, sport, or business. It might be anything that you feel strongly about. It will always be something that will propel you out of your comfort zone into action, and it will always involve change in either a small or big way.

Be careful: your friends and family members may begin to label you as crazy and abnormal and weird, when it is they, instead, who are living their lives in the abnormal default setting, disengaged and dead. They are dead to ideas, creativity, vision and innovative thinking. And this is because they have not yet stumbled upon what drives them. They have not discovered their passion.

Find the Passion!

In differentiating between passion and love, passion is the driver. Love is more the thread that permeates the entire fabric. So, I can be passionate about a particular thing and it spurs me and it energizes me and it moves me to think and do whatever that passion might be. This applies to anybody. It is not unique to any one person. Ninety-nine and 44/100 percent of people are capable of love. And if you love, you can develop a passion. This is the reason why I have written this book—to inspire the leader that is in you to elevate you from the ordinary to the extraordinary.

Love is a part of that. We often hear love and passion, passion and love. In many ways, they go hand-in-hand. I think that you cannot be passionate about something if there is not love for that thing. I don't know that you can love without being passionate about something. So, passion is definitely a component of love.

Let's take the great California redwoods. There are people who would tell you, "I love the environment." They're tree huggers. And they're very passionate about the environment. And it goes on from there.

Sierra Leone Children's Scholarship Fund

One of the things I am passionate about is the Sierra Leone Children's Scholarship Fund that I created. I am passionate about children because of their simplicity. And wrapped in their simplicity is their potential to do anything—and I mean anything—given proper nurture and environment.

I created the Scholarship Program in 2015 beginning with five students. Today there are 23 students in the program. There are two criteria to be met to be eligible for consideration: you have to demonstrate great financial need, and you need meet very high academic standards. These are the only two stipulations.

These children would not be able to go to school if they didn't get some kind of help. They come from very impoverished backgrounds. Their parents lack the finances to spend on education.

The children are required to write to me in their own handwriting. I ask them to tell me about themselves: "Do you have any siblings?" "What would you like to be when you grow up?" "Tell me about your parents." "What do you like?"

Now when you look at their report cards and their national exam scores, you'll see they're above average academically. Yet, in many instances, where they go to school, there is no electricity and no running water. Sometimes, three children share the same seat in a classroom.

Yet, they're doing well academically. Imagine if they had a little bit of help, how much better they could be! Once, when I was distributing scholarship money, one of the mothers cried. She said, "Many days my son goes to school without anything to eat." She is beside herself. Her son says, "Don't worry. I'll get some food from my friends." So, he mooches off his buddies. But his national exam scores are very high.

There are five boys in the program and 18 girls. My emphasis is on girls because I want to empower girls to feel and know that they have the potential to do anything. The limited number of boys in the program are selected for a reason as well. And that is, I want them to learn and understand that girls have as much to contribute to the conversation as boys do and they should always seek to include the female perspective in every discussion that they are involved in. A discussion or conversation that is overwhelmingly one-sided—either male or female in perspective, thinking, and experience—is not much of a conversation at all when it comes to results.

One hundred dollars a year covers their entire tuition. It's something I'm very excited about. It's like planting a seed and you never know how big that tree is going to grow. Once it grows, who else can they help? Who else can seek shelter under its branches?

The school that I'd like to build will be called the Hope School. It will be very small at 50 students per grade level: elementary, junior high school, and high school. It will be fully automated with the focus on leadership. The school week will be six days and the school day ten hours long—and everything will be accomplished in that time, including all classroom work, homework assignments, study, sports, and environmental (volunteer) activities. When they're cut loose, they're on their own time with their small group leader (SGL). At the foundation there will be children doing their reading, writing, and arithmetic as well as other core subjects like history and social studies. There will be functional subjects that are different from the core subjects—subjects such as language, arts (music, dance, and fine arts), sports, and leadership—that every student will take each year. Mentoring and coaching will be done on a continuous basis twenty four hours a day and seven days per week. I envision dormitory style rooms with class leaders. This is the military school model. The typical class size will be about 12 students. Each of those students in a group will have an adult leader, an SGL, who stays with them 24/7, even in their sleeping quarters.

Now that I'm retired from the military, that's the next phase that I'm focusing on.

A Challenge is Just a Speed Bump

A speed bump slows me down. But it's not intended to stop me. That's the way I see challenges.

Continuous and consistently clean drinking water, routinely clean power, adequate and corruption-free security and automation are all challenges for third world countries. I'm not quite ready to build the school as I envision it at this moment. But there is certainly a need for one. In the meantime, I can utilize the current infrastructure and still support the children.

My objective is to help children. So all I needed to do was to identify a vehicle to do so. Well, once I broke it down like that, I realized that there were many types of vehicles that I could use to get to my destination, which is to help children.

Imagine this classroom: dirt floors, a light hanging by a wire, and three butts in one chair! How can you learn if you're hungry? How can you learn if your environment isn't conducive to it?

This is my passion! What is yours? Allow your search to begin.

Can You Help?

You may already be familiar with the African proverb, "If you want to go fast, go alone. If you want to go far, go together." I'm looking to enlist others with a similar passion as mine. I'm working from the premise that I'm doing this alone and I have to start it alone. But I'm sure there's help out there. If you'd like to lend a hand, it would be very much appreciated!

It is my inspiration to help children. But my inspiration is selfish. I'm not being altruistic, but instead I take the position that I must do this because I don't have a choice. Even if it seems selfish to some, I (and we) must do this. It is paramount for our children.

The following was written by an anonymous author about our progeny and I paraphrase: Because they will sit where we are sitting, and when we are gone, attend to those things we think are important. We may adopt all the policies we please, but how they will be carried out depends on them. They will assume control of our cities, states, and our nation. They are going to build our homes and take over our churches, mosques, synagogues, temples, schools, and corporations. All our work is going to be judged, praised, or condemned by them. The fate of humanity is in their hands. So, it might be well to spend some time and effort on them and educate them well.

The late Nelson Mandela wrote that "Our deepest fear is not that we are inadequate. Our deepest fear is that we are powerful beyond measure." Passion obliterates fear. Passion is the antidote to fear. Passion is personal.

What is Your Essence?

If you take away only one thing from this book, I hope it will be the following: Don't do anything if you are not passionate about it, and don't do any type of work that you are not passionate about. When you fail to pursue your passion, you will not have integrity with yourself. The result is that you compromise and then settle for what is. When you do this, you have stopped living, and when you are not alive, you are dead. It is not a coincidence that we refer to people in this mode of life as zombies or robots.

I would encourage you to identify this passion and make a decision to act on it, knowing that it's not unique to anybody else but you. It is something that you have within you and it doesn't cost you anything. You don't need to go buy it at Walmart. You come built and hardwired with it.

When you are engaged with your passion, you tap into the deep and endless well of creativity and become innovative; you experience timelessness and effortlessness in doing it, and at that point you begin to live. You begin to live because you no longer recognize and are bound by time. You become innovative because you think differently in endless ways about how to do what you are passionate about. You experience effortlessness because you do not consider it work. It flows, it feels right, and you are never tired because only you can do it the way you do it. While others may try, it's not quite the same as when you do it, because when you do it, you achieve the "Wow!" factor. You are alive and nothing else matters.

I think we all understood what Dr. King meant when he said, "It doesn't matter anymore." He was not worried about his life. It was as if he was saying, "You can shoot me now, it doesn't matter. The horse is out of the barn." And I think when you get to that point, you become transformed, and then you become lethal in your quest and in your passion for something. You start to think about it differently and now there's a cause, a purpose. You are the only one on point out there, alone.

***

PART 3

OTHER ELEMENTS OF GOOD LEADERSHIP

While the four pillars (CLIP) I have just mentioned are paramount, there are other factors that contribute to successful leadership. These items—listening, alertness, exceeding standards, decisiveness, education, teamwork and motivation, mentorship and diversity, generational issues and multi-domain leadership—are part and parcel of what influences people.

These are the mortar and consistency of the four pillars. Without them, the pillars won't stand up. They crumble to the ground.

For a sampling of the chapters ahead, consider:

- President Calvin Coolidge said that "No man ever listened himself out of a job." Saying dumb things doesn't happen when you're listening.
- We get text alerts and spoiler alerts—but do we ever really stop and think about what the word "alert" means? It is similar to, but not exactly the same, as readiness.
- In this "everybody gets a trophy" world we live in, are we doing people a disservice? Are we setting them up for failure by coddling them? Shouldn't they want to go "above and beyond" in all that they do?
- We all appreciate squirrels who are decisive and get out of the way when we're driving. He who hesitates is lost.
- Education is key to a civilized society. Yes, education costs money. But then so does ignorance.

- Teamwork and motivation are essential to cooperation, harmony and unity. When people get along, the whole is greater than the sum of the parts.
- Mentorship and diversity are fundamental to the developmental world.
- Generations need to see eye-to-eye if progress is to be made.
- The concept of multi-domain leadership is the next level that we need to get to in order to compete in a changing world.

All these items should be taken into consideration when considering the all-encompassing subject of leadership—whether in the business world, the military, or society in general.

CHAPTER 11
Listening

"Wisdom is the reward you get for a lifetime of listening when you'd have preferred to talk."—Doug Larson

I would say that among the traits that I have found good leaders possess, the following 10 qualities are a pretty thorough list: Patience, competence, fairness, respect for self and others, listening, developing strategy, vision, ability to develop long and short-term goals, prioritizing and making decisions. In this chapter, I would like to focus on listening, the forgotten skill.

While not technically one of my Four Pillars of Leadership, the ability to listen is a key element of competent leadership. Effective listening skills equate to being a powerful leader. I like quiet leaders. They have checked their egos at the door. Quiet leaders possess three very unglamorous virtues: restraint, modesty, and tenacity.

Many people think the opposite of talking is waiting to talk. It's not. It's listening.

That's Why He'll Always Be King to Me

When I was a new officer, I learned a great deal from Command Sergeant Major (CSM) Joe Boledovic. As you may know, by the time you get to be a CSM, you've got about 30 years in the military—so he'd been around the block more than once. Generally, CSMs are older and convey a bit of a grandfatherly advice to very young officers—as I was at the time. Even though I have retired, I still consider him to be a close friend and he is MY COMMAND SERGEANT MAJOR (caps are used for emphasis; I trusted him with my life).

One of the things I became known for was that I liked to go out into the field. I didn't like to stay in the armories during drill weekends. Whenever we assembled, I would have training opportunities somewhere away from the base.

One weekend, we took a road trip to Fort Dix. We would camp out in the field at a bivouac site at night and utilize some of the facilities on post (the Army base) as well. The reservists would work at their civilian jobs during the day, so they generally wouldn't arrive until after dark on Friday evenings, after they'd reported to the armory, gotten into uniform, and been shuttled to the location.

I was just coming on board as a leader this particular weekend and was therefore in charge of the operation. On these excursions, we used our own equipment. That included land navigation training (for example, we used our own vehicles and weapons), or we would do weapons qualification or some other activity.

From Yonkers, the route down to Fort Dix was to cross the George Washington Bridge, then take Interstate 95 south to Exit 7B. One of the things we were bringing with us was a mobile kitchen trailer (MKT), which is basically a kitchen on wheels, and includes a stove and a refrigerator; so everything is compact in one unit and is designed to prepare meals for about 300 service members.

I had gone on ahead as part of an advanced party with six to seven other team leaders from various sections to attend what is known as "range control," where we would receive a briefing, then sign for everything we were going to use during the duration, including the bivouac site, the bathroom facilities, the dining room facilities, and any other support we needed. We also set up tents and handled other administrative tasks.

What I didn't know was that our MKT was left on the highway. Somehow, the trailer became unhitched and it was in a million pieces all over 95 South. I didn't find out about it until the following morning.

That night, I was kept up until the early hours of the morning by CSM Boledovic, who, to put it mildly, liked to talk. This guy just didn't sleep. He was a freakin' machine when it came to conversation! However, you just don't know how much I appreciated those talks—he would impart wisdom all night long.

At about 4 a.m., I heard a knock on my tent. It was one of the cooks, who said, "Breakfast is going to be late." He went on to tell me the MKT was a no-show. I asked him, "Why don't we have the

MKT?" And that's when I heard about the MKT becoming unhitched and breaking up on the highway. The cook said they only retrieved parts of it but they weren't able to put it back together. He and the other cooks didn't find out about it until 1 a.m., when they got up to begin to prepare breakfast for the 170 people on ground.

As I thought about the consequences of what happened, the CSM said, "I can hear the wheels spinning in your head. Take a nap. Sleep for an hour. I'll make sure you get up." I dozed off, naively hoping that a resolution would appear out of thin air.

While I slept, CSM Boledovic checked into the situation. He got the full story. He came back, woke me up, and said, "Hey boss, here's the full deal." He explained what happened and said, "We'll deal with headquarters later on." He and I both knew the implication was that I had 170 soldiers who had been sleeping out in the woods. It was about 35 degrees outside and it appeared as if they weren't going to have any breakfast—not even a cup of coffee—before they started their day.

One Shining Moment

Soon it would be time for assembly (formation). I'll never forget what CSM Boledovic said to me. He said, "What you do right here, right now, at this moment, is going to determine whether these soldiers will EVER listen to you again." My head was spinning and I didn't know what to do, all because I was just finding out about this dilemma.

CSM Boledovic saw my predicament, came over to me, and put his arm around my shoulder. I said, "What have you got?" He said, "It's cold out here, you've got soldiers and you've got to feed them before the day starts." I was well aware of that! I asked him what ideas he had.

He said, "There's a Burger King on post. You've got trucks. Lots of trucks. You've even got a bus." He pulled $100 out of his pocket, slapped it into my hands, and said, "Feed these soldiers." Without even starting to think about it, I quickly summoned my driver, jumped into my Humvee and drove to the nearest ATM. My limit was $300, which I promptly withdrew, then headed for the Burger King on post and asked for the manager.

I told him, "In about 40 minutes about 170 soldiers are going to show up. They will each get a cup of coffee and a breakfast sandwich.

Here's $400 to start. I'll circle back with you to find out if you need more." I gave him my phone number and told him I'd be back shortly.

Bottom Line

The upshot of the whole episode is that I learned an invaluable lesson about how to handle soldiers. I did not learn it at the academy. I didn't learn it in a basic or an advanced course. I learned it from an experienced, seasoned senior NCO.

Even now, guys who were privates at the time will see me and say, "You are the man! We'll follow you anywhere." Apparently, they all knew what had happened. No one had any idea what they were going to have for breakfast that day, if anything.

I still keep in touch with CSM Boledovic. He was a bus driver in Queens, New York. He spoke quite a few languages. We're still friends. I still call him every now and then and pick his brain. He is a fine gentleman and an outstanding human being.

When I thanked him, he said, "I didn't do anything differently for you that I wouldn't have done for any other officers I served with. The only difference was that you listened."

Mr. Bacci, the chairman from the Curtis High School science department said the same thing back in 1981 when I graduated. I was not the valedictorian but I won lots of science awards: the International Science and Engineering Fair, General Electric Science award, Junior Engineer Technical Society award, B'Nai B'rith for community service, and money in the form of checks.

After being endlessly called to the stage for one award after the other, the chairman told the audience of families, friends, and graduates the same words I heard from the CSM. Mr. Bacci told the parents, "We in the science department did not do anything differently for Dan Harris than we did for all of the other students. The only difference is that Dan Harris listened." Slow to speak, and first to listen is another of the traits I learned from my grandfather, Pedro, in Liberia before emigrating to the United States in February 1977.

The lyrics from the Simon and Garfunkel song, "The Sound of Silence" resonated with me—especially when they sang, "...people talking without speaking, people hearing without listening, people writing songs that voices never share..."

Many Equate Being Listened to as Being Loved

Hearing is one of the five senses. But listening is an art. It is more cognitive and therefore requires more effort.

Communication is hard work. And listening is not a passive activity. Asking good questions and listening is one of the best ways I know of to communicate effectively.

I once read a quote by Dr. Paul Tournier that I felt summed up the topic nicely. Tournier said, "It is impossible to overestimate the immense need humans have to be really listened to, to be taken seriously, to be understood."

***

CHAPTER 12
Alertness

"An ounce of prevention is worth a pound of cure." —Ben Franklin

John Wooden, the late, great (legendary) basketball coach of the UCLA Bruins basketball team described alertness as to "be observant and eager to learn and improve." In fact, it was one of the cornerstones in his Pyramid of Success.

Protecting, keeping an eye out, anticipating and looking at the big picture, and putting into place things to mitigate disaster are all tenets of effective leadership.

Wouldn't business leaders want to know what's coming up? Wouldn't politicians? Investors would certainly like to know what's going to happen—so they can invest their money accordingly. A good leader is always looking ahead, anticipating, and developing courses of action and wargaming them.

The word "paranoia," even though it has a negative connotation, could be defined as "a heightened state of awareness," such as being on guard. Is that so bad? Is it wrong to think of the future periodically, instead of the past and the present all of the time? A leader should encourage short as well as long-term goals and thinking.

Unfortunately, a lot of what we do today is reactionary. An event takes place and we react. This is naïve. The world has changed. America is a superpower and the envy of much of the rest of the world. Therefore, many people want to bring us down. That's the cold, hard reality.

Having your antenna up is a good leadership tenet. But regrettably, that's not always the norm. Henry Ford said, "Thinking is the hardest work there is, which is why so few people do it." I encouraged junior commanders on my team to do two things: the first was to make time to read about their profession and the second was to make time to think about their profession and how to improve upon it and do things differently.

Mr. Ford was correct. Thinking is hard work indeed because you have to quiet your mind and dismiss all of the other irrelevant noise from your brain.

Expect the Unexpected

Even if the probability of an event happening is so far afield from what you would think, you should still develop mitigating measures.

A leader might say, "At this point, I'm anticipating this scenario," or, "Currently I'm encountering this. Here are two or three courses of action I think we should take, and 'Oh, by the way this is my recommended approach.'" For me, this is a huge part of leadership. When you are the boss, this should be the dance that takes place between leading and following.

Owning and operating at those levels—where you're constantly thinking through these issues—is tantamount to effective leadership. Constantly conjuring up scenarios and working through concerns is imperative if you want to call yourself a leader and be persuasive.

Don't Get Caught Flatfooted

You don't want to have an "oh shit" moment. If you do, it's too late and you have failed your duty as the boss. You should never be surprised as a leader. In the Army we used to say, "Surprises are for birthdays, so don't surprise me."

When you have 10 people on your team, I guarantee you all 10 will be different and that's an asset to be leveraged against any problem. No two of them will be alike. I have often heard that when two people agree on everything, one of them is unnecessary. Getting them to push or pull in the same direction requires patience. Professionally, tactfully, and respectfully disagreeing—backed by facts, reason, and experience—is always welcome and appreciated. Great followers should never hold back, even if it is unsolicited.

I want people on my team to alert me and say something if I'm wrong. What I'm looking for is someone who will think about the opposite of what I say and am ready to do—and offer the opposite perspective. This is a reminder that intelligence is the ability to associate two totally opposite and different things and then arrive at a conclusion or synthesis. I want them to remember that, and I need them to not just nonchalantly give me their thoughts and opinions about it. I need them to have a "jump on my desk" moment.

What I mean by this is to walk into my office, climb up onto my desk (while I'm sitting there), reach down and grab me by the ears, look me in the eye and say, "Boss! You need to ____." Do whatever you need to do to get my attention! I need them to operate from that perspective and mindset. If they need to grab me by the lapels to wake me up, it could very well be worth the humiliation.

I don't want people waiting to tell me that there's a problem until it's grown to be so colossal and obvious that I have to react immediately. When we're both standing at the edge of a hole and we're going to hell in a handbasket and you tell me, "Hey boss, we have a problem," then, at that point, you are of no use to me. I'm probably going to look at you and push you in the hole myself. I have eyes. I can see for myself that we have a problem. It's pointless to tell me now that we have a problem!

Forewarned is Forearmed

The genius is for you to have anticipated, foreseen, and advised about the situation before we arrived at the hole. Where were you 30, 60, 90 days ago? Where were you six months ago? An effective leader should anticipate that they have to deal with A, B and C because they looked at the battlefield and assessed the situation.

I want team members to present the situation to me for my consideration and follow it up with, "Oh, by the way, this is my recommended course of action." If you can do this with your boss, you are actually serving them. You need to anticipate challenges in order to prevent or to mitigate the impact. If you can't avert outcomes, you need to mitigate them. There is always something that can be done.

When I was in command, I always shared with the staff that, "It may come as a surprise to you, but I do listen to you. You are important. I want to hear from you. I want to know what you think."

Always Ready, Always There

I spent 30+ years in the Army National Guard. Many people don't know, specifically, what the National Guard is, or does. As mentioned earlier, they do a variety of things, not the least of which is to protect the country from the proliferation of nuclear, biological, and chemical weapons and high-yield explosive devices. The Guard also gets involved in things such as drug enforcement and money laundering by working with civilian agencies.

There are three components of the armed forces: active, reserves, and the National Guard or militia. The tagline of the National Guard is, "Always Ready, Always There."

The Guard began as citizen soldiers in Massachusetts in 1636. With the passage of federal legislation in 1903, the militias officially became the National Guard. Article 1, Section 8 of the U.S. Constitution recognized the then existing state militias and gave Congress the power to call them out, "to execute the laws of the Union, suppress insurrections and repel invasions." The National Guard, unlike the other armed services, is commanded by the governor of their state under normal circumstances. The president, however, can "federalize" them, where he (or she) becomes their commander-in-chief. The National Guard is all about alertness.

***

CHAPTER 13
Don't Just Meet Standards, Exceed Them

"Ah, but a man's reach should exceed his grasp. Or what's a heaven for?" —Robert Browning

Admirable leadership traits, some implicitly touched on earlier, include transparency, learning from failure, trust, confidence, humility and creativity. I'd like to drill down further by devoting chapters to exceeding standards, decisiveness, education, teamwork, and motivation as well as mentorship and diversity. I'll also address what is called "multi-domain leadership." Once again, these should all be conducted using courage, integrity, passion, and love.

Effective leaders are focused on the extraordinary. When I go back to the military and am talking with officers charged with giving awards, I say there's a simple criterion for deciding whether or not an individual has earned an award: the individual must have exceeded the standards, not just met them. So, for example, while on active duty, we took the APFT (Army Physical Fitness Test) twice a year, every six months.

The optimal score on APFT is 300. It involved the following things: push-ups, sit-ups and a two-mile run. The minimum passing score is 180 points. I'm frustrated when leaders come to me and want to give a soldier an award for getting 180 points. That's what the soldiers are supposed to do! They're supposed to pass. You can shake the hand of everybody who did well and high-five each other and I'm fine with that. But don't give an award just for passing the test! The reward is in having passed.

I have also argued that you don't even give an award for maxing the test. You give an award for the guys who went ABOVE max scale (there is an extended scale for those soldiers who went above the score of 300 points in their age category). And we had people who would. They would get above 300. In their age categories, they scored 315, 336, or 350. Those guys and gals should be awarded. They've exceeded the standard. Leadership, in my mind, is always working to get your people to exceed standards—not to just meet them.

Complacency and Comfort

In my thinking, comfort is a bad thing. I read a quote once that said, "The point on the thermostat where it is neither hot nor cold is called a comfort zone." I would argue that, in fact, it's the dead zone. Because when you're comfortable, your creative mind is not working, you lose initiative, and you stop being bold. You fail when you do not take the initiative to get up and do something. It is well known that you will not exercise boldness in doing anything when you're comfortable. You are "status quo." The result of all that is complacency, where the expectation—or the status quo—will just continue on.

Leaders should not encourage comfort and complacency. It's the worst thing that they can do. They need to lead their people away from that. If you find that your people are in that area or that space, get them out of it! You want them to be working creatively. You want them to be innovative. You want them to demonstrate courage. You always want your people to be leaning forward and taking the initiative.

A good example of how that can happen is in the way I define the Army as "America's army." What's the purpose? It is simply to fight and win America's wars. Period. And we do so by being on offense! We may transition into defense to do a few things: rest, refit, refuel, get supplies, etc.

But make no mistake, the U.S. military's arsenal in the pack is that we are constantly on the move. We win our fights by being on the offense and not the defense. We will pursue the enemy. We will go after them. We don't sit and wait. And we win in this fashion. We do this by taking the initiative and moving forward—not sitting back and being comfortable.

I'm not saying it's always, "Go go go go go go go!" No! There are times in your forward movement that you are going to have to transition into a defensive posture.

But it's a transition. And immediately you switch back into that offense where you're pursuing the objective. And I think effective leaders employing that tactic in the civilian realm, in business applications and leadership positions, can also be successful that way.

So comfort and complacency are negatives. Don't embrace them! It's easy to do so—and too many people have a tendency to do that which is easy.

***

CHAPTER 14
Be Decisive

"In any moment of decision, the best thing you can do is the right thing. The worst thing you can do is nothing." —Theodore Roosevelt

Effective leaders make timely decisions. One of my greatest frustrations when I was in the Guard was when I needed a decision from my boss and he would say, "Oh, I'll get back to you tomorrow." My initial thought was, "Dude, your only purpose in life is to make decisions! You can't make one now? The army pinned a star on you to make decisions, sent you to all kinds of schools and spent plenty of money to educate and train you! I need a decision on a dime and you can't make one. What good are you?"

Of course, that is not the proper way to address a leader—even a bad one. So I would keep my mouth shut but I would go back to my desk and go, "Arrrh." I realized his challenge was that he didn't want to put his ass on the line. That should never be a leader's problem. If as a leader, that is your concern, then you're probably not being genuine or truthful about something. I honestly feel that if you are truthful, honest, and genuine about a decision and the outcome is bad, you'll know that you made the best decision you could under the circumstances.

Trust me, they will let you know they think you were negligent, but that is why we have investigations. They will investigate, the truth will come out, and you'll be vindicated. You will learn from the mistake, and it will be catalogued and documented for others to learn from in the future. Extraordinary leaders should welcome and support investigations because the results add to the body of truth for the benefit of our collective future.

However, if they investigate and find out that you were disingenuous and you were nefarious in your dealings, and find out something was not on the up and up, the people will demand your head on a platter—and that's most likely why you were afraid of making the decision.

The takeaway is this: A "decision" is a neutral thing until it is applied to a problem or situation and we experience the outcome. Only after we frame the outcome do we apply a label to it as good or bad depending on what it was. But the decision itself, "Go" or "No go," is neutral and a decision based on courage, love, integrity, and passion will always yield extraordinary results.

Consistency is Key

In our society, we want consistency from our leaders. You are a good leader if you consistently make good decisions. They'll give you awards and ribbons, and you'll get your picture in the newspaper. They'll even give you parades! It's okay to make one bad decision. Just don't make a habit of it!

If you're a leader who consistently makes bad decisions, you'll be skinned alive. It's just what happens. It's not good or bad. It's just what it is.

You're expected to leverage all of your knowledge, your gut instinct, and all the things you have done well. You're also expected to leverage your relevant stakeholder's input and feedback through thorough collaboration and coordination.

It's also normal to make quick calculations. That's why you're paid the big bucks, for being the leader. Even though it may be this hasty, fly-by-the-seat-of-your-pants thing, if you need a decision quickly, that's okay.

The bottom line is leaders should not be afraid to make decisions.

***

CHAPTER 15
Get Educated

"I never teach my pupils. I only provide the conditions in which they can learn." —Albert Einstein

One thing I do now to help fine-tune leadership in our society is teach in the graduate school of business at Mercy College, which is located in Dobbs Ferry, New York. The Masters of Science in Organizational Leadership (MSOL) is an excellent and diverse program. Sometimes when the schedule allows and we have enough students interested, we take the classes out on cover field trips and do things like climb a mountain and talk.

One time we met at the Delaware Water Gap at the intersection of New York, New Jersey, and Pennsylvania. It's in the Poconos and the students were very impressed with it. They could've stayed in their bedrooms on campus on a Saturday morning as most students typically sleep until 10 or 11 a.m. But here they were, ready to summit this mountain.

One of the first things I suggested to my students on my day is that they should always value their time. That's what I do. If I'm going to spend my time listening to someone, they had better give me something worthwhile. Whatever else I'm going to do with my time is very valuable to me. In some ways, the only thing that we have is our time.

Start With Why

I also posed a question to the group of students to get them thinking, "Why are you going to business school?" Answers ranged from, "My grandfather did business and his father was in business before him," to "Well, I can make a lot of money." True. You can make a lot of money stealing, but you're not stealing because you can make a lot of money, so why're you doing business? In response to this further prodding, I got, "I enjoy business. I like the idea of doing business."

All the answers did not touch on what I was looking for. So I kept asking the question, "Why did you study undergraduate business?" It really got them thinking as we were engaging this mountain. And it took us about three hours to climb.

Do Something That You Like to Do, Please

We got up to a nice area where we were sitting on rocks and overlooking the gap and it's a spectacular view. They asked why I was teaching this class. I told them when I was an undergrad I couldn't even spell business. If you paid me, I wouldn't touch it. But that's because I wasn't ready back then, and now I am and I'm doing it because it's my choice.

And then one young lady said that, "I'm doing business because I choose to do business." That's it! It's your choice. It's the power of your choice!

I was insinuating that they not get bogged down and overburdened with their family legacy if that is not what they wanted to do. Whatever you do is a bad thing if you're doing it because someone wants to live vicariously through you. But if it's your choice, you are free to create and do variations on it.

Do something different and innovative if you're not busy trying to carry this burden of a legacy that was handed down to you from your family. That is the first thing you need to look at. Ask yourself, "Is this my choice?" And immediately after answering that with a resounding, "Yes," your passion will take over. And when passion kicks in, creativity steps in, innovation steps in and your thinking becomes different about that very thing.

Lord knows we have enough businesspeople in the world already. I want you to find your passion.

One important question, however, is, "How sure are you that this is your passion?" I know that when you are doing something you're passionate about, you will begin to experience two things. The first is timelessness. An outrageous (but not entirely unbelievable) example is you're thinking it's seven in the morning when actually it's three-thirty in the afternoon (or vice versa).

Second is effortlessness. It just flows. You may have to move a ton of stuff and you do it without breaking a sweat. So it's effortless and it's timeless. When you experience these two things while you're doing something, you know you are hardwired to do it.

Another Road Trip

In the future, I'm taking another group of students to the Berkshire mountains in Massachusetts, just east over the New York border. I've partnered with a very good friend of mine named Eyal Shapira. He is president of the Raritan Central Railway in Raritan, New Jersey. Eyal once honored me with an introduction at a gathering with these few words, "As you know, most great Americans were not born in America. Ladies and gentlemen, let me introduce you to Lieutenant Colonel Dan Harris." I am still moved and inspired by his words.

Eyal is an Israeli-American gentleman who loves America, loves the military, and supports our armed forces with every ounce of blood in his veins. Eyal used his wealth and resources to purchase more than 272 acres, which he calls Pugzee Farm, named after his dog (sadly, I learned during my work on this book that Pugzee passed away). On the other side of his property in the Berkshires is Arlo Guthrie's family home.

Eyal went to Coronado, California, which is where the Navy SEALs candidates conduct Phase 1 Basic Underwater Demolition (BUD). He petitioned for the blueprints for a leadership reaction course with a retired Navy commander, Captain Drew Bisset. Independent of the Navy, Captain Bisset and his team established a SEAL RDAC (Recruiting District Assistance Council) program in Connecticut where they prequalify candidates who are applying to become Navy SEALs before they get to the actual program. There are several other programs like it around the country, but Captain Bisset and his team are the ones who have achieved the highest graduation rate in the U.S. Their success rate is 70 percent (against numbers of 10 percent, 13 percent, and 17 percent). They've clearly cracked the code, with intense leadership and physical training. The candidates bring the grey matter and their willingness.

My students come from all walks of life. One of them has his

PhD from Yale and one of them was a fireman. Who knows, some of them may develop a desire to serve mother America in the Navy SEALs—or a similar elite military force (e.g., the Marines have Force Recon, the Army has the Rangers, Green Berets, and Delta force) for the various services. I assure them if they join, it's going to be leadership intensive.

I tell them: There are a million investment analysts and brokerage agents out there, working for very sexy salaries. Are you just going to be another one added to that pool? What's unique about you?

These interactive experiences with graduate and undergraduate students are fitting and valuable. We did the Delaware Water gap in the past. We're going to Pugzee farm in the future. And we have other venues where I intend to instill the principles of leadership in them.

***

CHAPTER 16
Teamwork and Motivation

"... he would never ask his players to do what he wouldn't do. You appreciate that, when the leader is willing to get right out there and work alongside you. You're not just hearing stuff from somebody who hasn't been there and done it. He knew what he was talking about, so he had that credibility. He got respect."—Kareem Abdul Jabbar, about Coach John Wooden

A team should be like a family. Camaraderie is an amazing thing—it creates a chemistry that makes people do incredible things for each other. It is interesting how we remember the camaraderie, but don't remember the work involved. Helen Keller said, "Alone we can do so little. Together, we can do so much."

Albert Einstein said that "it is more important to focus on how you treat people rather than revel in who you know and who knows you." Doing for others comes naturally to people. We are hard-wired for this. Doing differently causes your body and your brain to short-circuit, because it is not the right thing. As Dr. Martin Luther King said, "The time is always right to do what is right."

Partnerships result in meaningful collaborations. Meaningful collaborations result in people putting out their best performance and product. There is power in people. It is important not to marginalize them.

Protection

A strong leader is like a big rock that provides you great cover in a firefight. You can return fire while seeking protection to figure out your next temporary move. This is such an important point that if you do not have that cover, you could lose your life.

Leadership is also the art of motivating people to act toward achieving common goals. Brinksmanship is the art of pushing a confrontation to the limit of safety to force a desired outcome. One is persuasive, the other coercive. One feels like success; the other, failure.

Drive

Daniel Pink said it well in his book *Drive*. He said that people in the workforce are motivated by three things: autonomy, mastery, and purpose. In other words, they like to have some say in the matter (autonomy); they need to feel like they are competent and good at what they do (mastery); and they need to feel that they are working for something greater than themselves (purpose).

All three simultaneously are not always possible in the military. At best you can experience one. And that's because you don't have as much autonomy in the military as you might have in the corporate world. It's very much prescriptive. And while the military does give you mastery in whatever you do, purpose has to come from your leaders.

Truly, the intent is to develop, think creatively about, and come up with ways of doing things that are going to better people and leave them more improved than when you met them. If you can do that, you're positively having an impact on people's lives.

I had an exercise for my children when they were growing up, which was to complete two assignments. I said, "I'm not worried about you getting all A's in school. You can fail every class." My daughter looked at me and said, "Yeah, you'll kill me." I said, "No, I'm not going to kill you. Don't worry about getting A's because more important are the two things I want you to concentrate on.

"The first thing is," I went on, "find out why you are here. There is a reason why you are here. Don't follow the humdrum of those that say, 'Oh, you're just born, you live your life and then you die.' There's meaning to your living. Find out what that is! There is something that only you can do the way you do it, such that it generates the 'Wow!' factor for people. You're the only one who can do it that way. Others may be able to do something similar—but it doesn't result in the 'Wow!' factor from people. Find out what's unique to you and you alone.

"And the other thing is, wherever you find yourselves, figure out how to improve the lives of the people you meet there. In other words, when you go somewhere either locally or around the world to meet people, don't leave them in the same condition that you met them. Do something to help improve their lives. If you do that," I continued, "grades are the least of your worries. They'll just fall into place."

I used to challenge them with those two thoughts, and with the thought process that "anything can happen." My daughter, my youngest, said, "Dad, do you mean anything can happen?" "Yes," I said, "Anything can happen." She would then invariably say, "You mean a big truck could fall down out of the sky? Wow!"

Of course for me, that mindset is biblically based, which says, "With God, all things are possible."

But effective leaders tease this feeling out of their people. They massage it out of those they encourage. They persuade, cajole, and coax—whatever words you want to use to get people to get it out of them.

Because we each have our strengths and weaknesses, and I honestly believe that I need to use my strengths to augment my neighbors' weakness. He, in turn, uses his strength to augment his neighbor's (or my) strengths and weaknesses, and so on and so forth.

I feel the purpose of life and why God made us with very different strengths is so that we complement each other and come to the full realization of how good that makes us feel and what we can realize. And until we do that, we're walking blind. It's not a coincidence that the feeling that you get when you help another person is euphoric and it generates a look that's priceless.

That's the way we're hardwired. That's why we're made. That's what we're supposed to do. It's effortless. It takes more effort to not help someone than to help them. This speaks to that love of other people that is one of the four pillars. You can't lead people if you don't love them.

***

CHAPTER 17
Mentorship and Diversity

"A mentor is someone who allows you to see the hope inside yourself."—Oprah Winfrey

I have advocated that we need to change the approach that is used now for mentorship. This is big for the Army. I'll stick to my lane, so I won't speak for the Navy, Air Force, Marines, or the Coast Guard.

Mentorship

All senior leaders must find junior leaders that they are mentoring. Great mentors teach and coach. They provide guidance, and guard you when you've done something stupid and need to cover. Great mentors work with you 24/7 both on and off duty. They see their mentee as their potential replacement somewhere in the Army.

Note, I did not say that juniors should approach seniors and request them to be mentors, as is the current practice. I remember being told, advised, and recommended on several occasions to seek out a senior officer at least two grades above my pay grade and ask them to be my mentor. For example, when I was a first lieutenant, I requested a lieutenant colonel to be my mentor and as a captain, I asked a colonel to be my mentor.

Of course, this system does not work because it is programmed to fail from the beginning. When I first heard about mentoring based on junior leaders approaching senior officers, it sounded like the most ass-backwards bullshit I had ever heard—and my skepticism proved to be well-founded when I tried it.

Of course, senior officers go on and on about mentoring. It briefs well on PowerPoint whenever general officers are present and talking to the rank and file. While it sounds great, the reality is very different.

To properly mentor a junior officer, senior officers will want to evaluate the junior for performance and potential. However, senior officers could not evaluate for potential because they did not have daily and regular visibility of that junior officer during their workday or night, on or off duty. This problem was compounded by the fact that junior officers often requested senior officers who were not in their chain of command to mentor them. Senior officers had little or no input for officers out of their chain of command.

But that's only the beginning of the problem. It is a human tendency to gravitate towards that which you know and feel comfortable with. The challenge is when you have such a diverse organization like the Army and you consistently have one group or type of individual at the lead.

It's a self-licking ice cream cone. Generally, most of the senior leaders are white men, typically coming from the same socioeconomic class. They like to play a particular type of sport. They probably have a preference for a particular type of drink. And they no doubt listen to a certain type of music. Pray tell me what type of mentees do you think these types of people feel comfortable having around them, or being with?

Clearly it's going to be like-minded people, right? Younger, like-minded people. So white junior officers who like that particular sport, who have developed or are developing a taste for a particular drink and listening to predictable kinds of music, or what have you, are most likely going to mesh well with senior officers.

Diversity

And most senior officers will not tolerate or even think of mentoring a young officer who talks differently, and has contrasting mannerisms and distant views. As a result, that type of individual will not get the benefit of the great mentorship, which means that you will find very few different people in those leadership positions.

It's a vicious cycle: lack of diversity in leaders leads to lack of diversity in mentees, which perpetuates the lack of diversity in leaders. It's because of the structure of this mentorship that we have. Senior leaders don't KNOW their junior leaders. That's why I say it needs to change. Until senior leaders become aware of and are comfortable with their mentees, this will be the status quo.

As with all things, there are exceptions and, in my experience, the exceptions all proved to be successful. As in the case with the six senior officers I mentioned previously, they mentored all of the officers who were in their chain of command. My peers and I did not have to request them to be our mentors. They found opportunities in everything to mentor, and in doing these activities, they imparted to me knowledge and experience.

They talked about opportunities. They explained some of their pitfalls, and so on. Senior leaders in the army are very busy people, but they always made time to talk. Colonel Dave Cox, an Air Force officer, was a prime example of this. He invited me into his office and told me to take a seat every time I knocked on his door. Then he leaned back in his chair, addressed my concern and answered my question and, most importantly, just talked.

The military is about leadership and mentorship. Leaders are supposed to mentor to prepare their replacements. But if a young officer does not get an opportunity to be in the sphere of influence of a senior leader, then we need to tweak the process. Mentorship is fundamental and there is a lot of talk about it, but it is marginalized and often inaccessible.

I will leave you in this chapter with this: Five of my 11 commanders were female, and the six males were a mix from the various ethnic groups. Trust me, differences didn't create a problem or lessen the quality of our work.

***

CHAPTER 18
Millennials vs. Boomers

"The generations of living things pass in a short time, and like runners, hand on the torch of life." —Lucretius

One of the things that I admire about our current generation of young people is the borderless, wall-less reasoning guiding their existence. They're not limited in their thinking—and to some extent there is no rulebook for them. Now that's good and bad. Bad in the sense that, for a person like me—who is structured—that turns me off. But I recognize some of the good in being the way they are.

For leaders to be effective, they must be cognizant and aware of the people on their teams. Today for the first time in our history we have up to five generations working in the same workspace and on teams.

You will have in your organization—to a lot lesser extent now, but you still have—a few of the old veterans or traditionalist people working. They've been doing so since the 1950s, some even since WWII. They were probably young teenagers when they started. Believe it or not, they're still out there working.

To that add your boomers, your Xers and then your millennials or Generation Y and even your post-millennials or Generation Z. As a team leader, you must recognize that you have this wide variety of people on your team and you need to understand that they have different motivations to work. Now if you don't have that recognition and you don't study and figure out how you're going to leverage those different generations for your project, your mission, and your objective, shame on you! Because what motivates an older veteran to work and spend that last teaspoon of blood in their veins on you is completely different from what motivates a millennial to do the same.

Part of my leadership approach is getting leaders to understand that different approaches are needed in today's workplace. Women—black women, white women and Asian women—have different motivations and things that empower them. As a leader, you need to know that, because you want to be able to leverage their talent and attributes in a positive way to achieve extraordinary results.

Time Marches On

What motivated a worker 40 years ago? They were defined by their work. If they were managers and supervisors, the position defined who they were. Recognition and prestige was (and is) important to them. To them it was a big deal to be obedient and have satisfying work. All of which are labels.

Go forward a little bit and the boomers and Xers are of the mindset that, "I have a corner office; I have a secretary; I have a parking space." Company loyalty and duty are big things for them. They go into the office with Brooks Brothers suits and Bruno Magli shoes. They have sleek haircuts. It's a big deal to walk in to see them. We are greeted by their executive assistants. Wow!

Gen Xers are more flexible, informal, and independent. Workplace diversity and work-life balance is important to them. In contrast, millennials don't even want an office. They don't even want to get dressed to go to work. You're not going to impress them with a parking space. Many of them don't even want cars. "I'll take a bike," or "I'll call Uber or Lyft," they say. You could try to tempt them with, "I'll give you a secretary!" "Thank you," they'll say, "but keep the secretary." They're not impressed by those things.

Clearly perks and signs of prestige are not motivating for them. Instead, they're inspired by causes. If they become aware that, "There is a campaign to save the yellow-tail spotted frog of Northwestern United States," they'll sign it. They'll send you checks. They're known to do that. They also seek growth and development. They are more global, entrepreneurial, and progressive.

Also, work must be fun, and they would like for you to get to know them personally. They want unique work experiences and they are not afraid to critique the quality of their managers.

It's important that leaders know who's on their team, what motivates these various groups of people, and how they as leaders can leverage these diverse motivations. That's integrity. That's what leadership is about.

If I'm the leader of the team and I know that you're all about saving the African elephant, I might consider sending you on vacation to Africa every year. Or send checks to those causes you care about. I would know this because I've taken the time to know my people.

"Hey, Nathan, we have this project A, B, and C that needs to get done. Oh, and by the way, it's typically around the time when you go to Africa for your vacation." As a leader, I'm very aware of that. And, "How is your affiliation with that group working with the elephants coming?" Talk about lighting up Nathan. "Oh yeah, it's great!"

Here's another motivating conversation for millennials. "I'm at a point where we have to ask you to help me out with this this time, but what I have done is gotten the financial officer's approval and the company is going to make a contribution to that cause of yours. Would you like that?" It could be something small like a $500 check. Do you think that employee would be walking on air? I think they would. And those types of actions are doable (and by the way, the company will get a tax write-off). So, these are some of the innovative, creative ways of leading people on your team to get them to produce extraordinary results.

Leadership Tool Bag

Another key thing for leadership is diversity of your leadership tool bag. I talk to students about this a lot. Effective leaders have a wide variety of tools in their leadership tool bag. And they carry that bag with them all the time. It is always hanging on their shoulders.

Here's an exercise I give my students at Mercy. I say, "Sit down and close your eyes. Imagine the biggest bag you can. It's your Santa Claus bag. You know that big bag that Santa carries around with him? It's similar, only yours is hanging around your shoulders. Put a sign on it, put a label on it. It's your leadership tool bag.

"Now, my challenge to you is, as you go through your day-to-day life—every time you read a book, every time you read an article, every time you hear a statement or something that resonates with you—capture it and put it in your tool bag. Those are the tools you're building. And when you have situations that you're facing that you've been anticipating and you know there are solution sets in your tool bag that you've collected, reach into that tool bag and leverage the solution set. How effective you're going to be depends on the variety of the tools you've packed in there."

I often think of Abraham Maslow's quote, "If the hammer is the only tool you have, you're going to look at everything as a nail." This makes so much sense. But not every problem is a nail. Some problems require just a staple. Others just a thumbtack. Yet there are problems that require you to use a chainsaw or stealth aircraft instead of an ordinary hammer.

In the military, you don't use a tank or a 9 mm round to shoot a fly. You don't need to employ a saber round from an M1 Abrams tank. It is overkill and will probably ruin everything around you. You don't need to drop a JDAM (Joint Direct Attack Munition) on a building when an RPG (rocket propelled grenade) would do the same thing. There's some finesse and competency required to be a leader, and a key to your success is knowing which tools to leverage on the problem you're facing.

The bottom line is to choose the tool that best fits the situation. The greater the diversity of tools in your tool bag, the greater the chance you will find just the right tool or set of tools.

Don't Force

Remember that when you're faced with a challenge, resist the urge to force a solution on it. A forced result would be something that doesn't fit. Or attempting to go against the grain or it's extremely difficult to achieve. Because ultimately when you do that, you don't solve that problem. You create a whole new one. And usually it's more complicated. Now it's become compounded. It is more difficult than what you were dealing with originally.

***

CHAPTER 19
Multi-domain Leadership

"The single biggest problem in communication is the illusion that it has taken place."—George Bernard Shaw

I now see an environment where many of our adversaries have gotten to be just as good as we are militarily. That's actually pretty scary. They do the same things we do equally well. Regarding technology, they leverage it very well. They recognize its importance so the question is, in a room full of equals, how do you stand out? What makes you different? What makes you able to fight and win?

If you're looking at students who all have top scores on the SATs and they're all valedictorians of their class and all have A's, well, then, okay what else have you got? And recognizing our role of the United States of America being the champion—being the one on point leading the so-called "free world"—how do we maintain that edge that we've always had when slowly but surely our adversaries are catching up to us?

What do you do differently? We started to look at this thing called multi-domain leadership. It's also called a multi-domain battle concept. It leverages psychological, emotional, and technological skills, and a broad range of things that the soldier does really well, at all levels. The expectation is that, "Joe Pound-It-on-the-Ground" can do this—can leverage psychological and emotional impacts to overcome his or her opponent. And that's the mindset.

Multi-domain leadership is a whole-person approach to leading against an opponent. I concede that my adversary is equally as smart as or better than me. So, I create opportunities to force him to take actions, thereby creating windows of vulnerability for him. I then can exploit and take advantage of the temporary windows of opportunity that I created. This requires a very resilient, flexible, and agile leader to be successful at operating in this manner.

The multi-domain leader has to simultaneously consider the domains such as time, space, globalization, environment, and culture (in addition to the usual concerns such as cyber) as windows of opportunities and vulnerabilities that open and close in each domain—singularly or in combinations of two or more. How can the average American use it? How can we use it in business? How can we use it in schools? How can we use it in families? It certainly is not going to be the same thing in each case—it's just a concept. How can we teach it to people so that they maintain the edge as well? I've given it some thought and I'm now developing a framework of how to apply the multi-domain concept to leadership.

We Don't Prepare Our Young Officers

As great as our military is, it has occurred to me that we do not prepare our young officers. When you become commissioned, you're a second lieutenant. All of us start that way. Whether it's the Air Force, Army, or Navy, you are a newly commissioned second lieutenant. And you get your commission either through the service academies (Annapolis, West Point or the Air Force Academy), through Reserve Officer Training Corp (ROTC) in colleges or schools, or Officer Candidate School (OCS) at Fort Benning, Georgia. Those are the ways in which you get commissioned. And the programs are for the most part prescriptive. You do your combination of academic college work as well as your military schooling and physical training. And at the end of this four-year period, you get your bachelor's degree and you're a commissioned officer.

But it has occurred to me that one topic or subject area that we're not doing enough of in preparing our young officers is the leadership piece, which is why I wrote this book. And that has become clear to me since we've been involved in this very long war on global terror. It's been going on 20 years and we're still going at it. And there is no foreseeable end.

And we have many young officers—leading men and women—who are leading people in these foreign remote places, with cultures and traditions that are very different from ours. Our culture here in the United States is very European-based, yet here we are serving in these places that are completely different—different places, different norms, different mores and different notions of what's right and wrong. And I don't think we are giving our young officers all of the leadership tools to help them to be successful.

Let me be clear on this. They're very well trained. They're very competent about their war-fighting capabilities. They've got that hands-down (or else we would not have a successful military). They know that. They're great Americans. But it seems to me that providing them with additional leadership tools—with an emphasis on additional leadership armor for their command bags, their soldier kit bags—would help them greatly.

So that's something I would like to see. And I've got to figure out how to have that conversation with the right people who are going to listen and buy into it. And the reason why I think that's important is because when I was in Iraq in 2004, I was with Operation Iraqi Freedom 3 (there was OIF 1, 2, 3, 3.5 and then it switched to New Dawn, Operation New Dawn, which concentrated more on nation-building and helping set up the countries' governments).

While there, I noticed there were many young people who were faced with challenges that were not military-related. It didn't have anything to do with what they faced or dealt with at West Point or in Annapolis or Colorado Springs. In many situations, they had to sit and talk to village elders, sheiks and imams, and negotiate about what resources you could bring to them to help them. And in many cases, they were talking to people who were old enough to be their grandfathers or great-grandfathers. So I felt a disparity there in experiential knowledge versus the academic book-type stuff.

They weren't just left out there to work on their own, of course. They had to come back and discuss things with the senior leaders and they would have protocols and all kinds of systems of checks and balances. But I think additional leadership tools in the bag would've helped to facilitate many of those discussions.

We always kept the 800-pound hammer sitting in the back, of course—the artillery or the QRF (quick reaction force). We'd say, "You are the village elder and we need to know, has anyone new moved into your village in the last 30 days?" Or, "Are you harboring insurgents?" And they would stall or not talk... or, "To hell with the Americans!" And if they refused to budge, at the end of the day I could always get on my phone and call in an air strike and this whole place would be leveled. That's just not the preferred method.

I felt these conversations would have gone differently, some more successfully than others, if some of the young officers had these additional leadership tools.

And there were some moral questions and issues as well. There was a lot of money flowing around Iraq—cash money, hard money, lots of money, real money. And many people, young and old, got themselves into a world of hurt because they didn't exercise good judgment.

By the time I deployed, I was already married, and had a son and a mortgage. So my perspective was different. Typically as a first lieutenant, you graduate college at age 21 or 22, so you're roughly a first lieutenant around 23 or 24. That's very young and you have this responsibility. You have a field ordering officer—that's the guy or gal who moves with cold, hard cash on the battlefield (they don't write checks or flip credit cards).

Let's say I roll into a town and in doing so I break one of your buildings with my tank, or I roll over your cow or plow through your cornfield. The field ordering officer jumps out and he's counting cash. A thousand dollars here, five hundred dollars there, two thousand dollars there! Not so fast!

The Army has a system for everything and that was not left to chance. But in those gaps of time between when the young officers would leave the location and do their reporting and their accounting and all the other type stuff, there was a lot of money out there that got a lot of people in trouble.

And I thought, if we had prepared many of these young people and some older people as well more for this type of example—of things that we face, perhaps—we wouldn't be surprised.

The Domains Get a Vote

If you want to effectively and successfully lead people, however, you can't ignore the four pillars of leadership. If you do, it will be to your detriment. Ultimately, people could lose their lives from bad decision-making.

In addition to the four pillars, there are other extenuating circumstances that play a part in decision-making and leadership. Hovering around the four pillars are domain elements such as culture, artificial intelligence, weather/temperature, cyber, space, land, sea, and sky.

The domains are not static, however. They are dynamic and they act independently to insert themselves into a leader's decision-making cycle for any length of time (or until the leader resolves the issue).

For example, every decision you make must take into account the culture of your organization. In addition, there's the culture of the geographic area where you are. A leader needs to think about all these factors. In America, it is illegal to accept bribes. In other cultures, it's not. Peter Drucker famously said, "Culture eats strategy for breakfast."

Even variables much less impactful and permanent than culture, such as weather elements, must still be taken into account when making a decision. For example, when it's 137 degrees outside, it gets your attention.

Elements are anything else that you need to consider in the equation. Unseen variables, such as the political climate—as well as psychological and spiritual warfare—add to the complexity of the leadership landscape.

The objective is always to either mitigate or eliminate variables. If you don't take into consideration all of the underlying circumstances, you can negatively affect the results you're looking to achieve. You really can't make a decision in a vacuum. You have to consider all of the elements.

The four pillars—CLIP plus Domain Medium plus Elements—lead to effective decision making, which leads people to achieve extraordinary results.

Effectively and Successfully Leading People

CLIP + Domain Medium + Elements => Effectively Leading People to Achieve Extraordinary Results

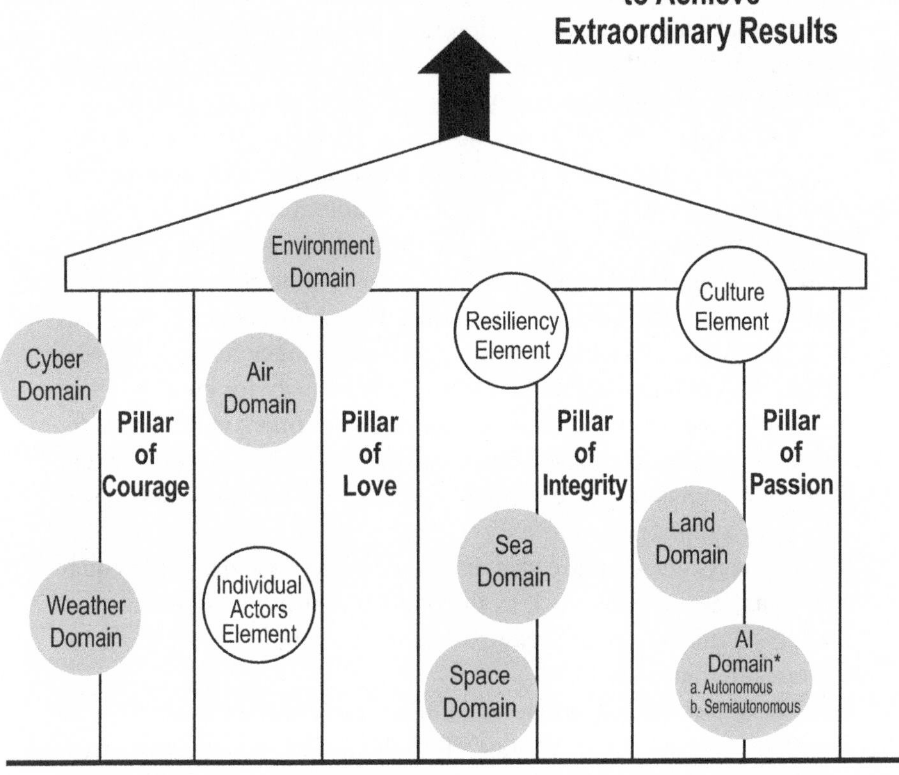

Figure 1

The **Multi-Domain Leadership Model** explains how to effectively and successfully lead people.
CLIP + Domain Medium + Elements => Effectively leading people to achieve extraordinary results.

---

*The AI Domain

Autonomous AI (Artificial Intelligence) is the most advanced form of AI. The processes are fully automated—and allow machines, systems, and robots to act on their own. It is totally devoid of human interaction and is independent of human intervention. Decision makers need to consider the element of autonomous AI.

Semi-autonomous Artificial Intelligence is a different form of AI. It is the second element in the Domain of AI. Semi-autonomous intelligence requires the confirmation of decisions by human operators. It does not act independently of human interaction. Decision makers will have to consider this element in their decision cycle or else their decision will not be based on the total amount of information available to them.

For example:
A person making a decision on an issue may decide differently—depending on whether they are involved with or considering autonomous AI or semi-autonomous AI.

PART 4

FIVE LEADERS SHOW THE WAY

I rated every senior officer I ever worked for until the last day I served in the Army. As a second lieutenant, I developed a simple table that I used to rate my senior officers. The criterion was simple. It came down to one item—selflessness—and I noted it by putting a simple X in a box. Although I never had a bad assignment in my 32 years in the Army, and every assignment was a great one, sadly, I cannot say the same about the many leaders I endured the pain to serve under. And, upon my retirement, I am all too happy to disassociate myself from ever knowing them. For many were such selfish and terrible people that, given a choice, I wouldn't follow them in the invasion of a McDonald's because they would get me killed by a flying frozen burger.

This next section reveals a little bit about the character of each of five individuals I encountered in my 32 years who were instrumental in my development as a leader. My encounters with some of these leaders were short-lived while others were prolonged, but the results were the same. They left a lasting impact on my personal and professional development.

Very simply, these individuals were selfless, and they were focused on one thing and one thing only: to get the Army's work done. They were not concerned about networking for themselves, politicking for themselves, making friends for themselves, or forming groups or cliques for themselves. Instead, they went about doing the Army's work and their business of soldiering selflessly.

You have already read about Captain Dan McNally in previous parts of this book. As you can tell, I have enormous respect for him. The following five military officers were also very influential in helping me to be the leader I am today.

Each and every one of them, in my opinion, has led with courage, love, integrity, and passion. The amount of courage that Captain Dan McNally displayed on 9.11 was exemplary. These next five officers, in their own inimitable ways, were equally as courageous, equally as passionate and equally as loving. And their integrity was (and is) commendable and honorable.

I have tremendous appreciation for them. In my opinion, this handful of great officers is one of the reasons why the American military is superior to other countries' armed forces.

CHAPTER 20
Colonel Stephanie Dawson

"Leadership is about making others better as a result of your presence and making sure that impact lasts in your absence."
—Sheryl Sandberg

Stephanie Dawson was an M-Day commander (a reserve commander), which meant she also had a full-time civilian job. She was Chief Operating Officer (COO) at the Port Authority of New York and New Jersey (a big organization with a lot of people, controlling a lot of money and impacting many lives).

Colonel Dawson was the first female sustainment brigade commander in the New York Army National Guard. To understand her position and responsibilities, it's helpful to understand the structure of the Guard. The highest level of the Guard is the *division*. Typically between three and five brigades make up a division. (In the modular concept, we have three types of Brigade Combat Teams, aka BCT, comprising armor, artillery, and infantry. Their sizes are increased or decreased, depending upon the mission set).

Between three and five battalions make up a *brigade*. Between three and five companies make up a *battalion*. Between 3 and 5 platoons make up a *company*. And between 3 and 5 squads make up a *platoon*. A *squad* is the lowest functioning element, and typically comprises two teams—an alpha team and a bravo team.

During the time I served under Colonel Dawson's command—first as operations and training officer, then as a battalion commander—I figured out that you can only effectively lead between three and five people at a time. You can lead more, but you're not going to be doing it well, at least not with the right quality and standards. And the quality and standards are two-fold, since leaders are evaluated and rated on performance and potential during a given period based on the seven Army values: loyalty, duty, respect, selfless service, honor, integrity, and personal courage (LDRSHIP).

There are other external policy-related items necessary for good order and discipline of the force, such as Sexual Harassment and Sexual Assault Response Prevention (SHARP), suicide prevention, antiterrorism force protection, physical security, certification compliance, etc. It dawned on me that the military created this structure and it works. If you allow everyone to do his or her job, everything will be fine. When things get out of whack with the chain of command, that's when it breaks down. Many in the Guard, even senior officers, don't get this.

Go Out of Your Way to Get a Key Decision Maker's Attention to Git-R-Done

Under Colonel Stephanie Dawson, I was a first operations/training officer, a key position (during peace time it is training; in a deployed situation, it's operations). I prepped everything for the staff.

Routinely, I had to get her review and approval of my work and often she would come into the office early before going downtown to her civilian office at 18th Street and Park Avenue. One time, when I had missed her in the office, she left to take the bus from 143rd Street and Lenox Ave. So I drove up with my stack of folders and said, "Ma'am. Come on, I'll give you a ride." She replied, "No, I'll take the bus." I said, "Get in." She did and no sooner had she fastened her seatbelt when I handed her the stack of folders with documents to look over and approve with her signature. She said "Oh, you're going to put me to work, huh?" I said, "I have to give you work when I can get you."

We laughed about it, but the bottom line was my job was to get what I needed done, done. She had a full-time job and therefore her time was at a premium. As a staff officer, you always have to adapt and be flexible around the decision maker or the leader. The purpose of the leader is to make decisions and I don't need her in the office for that. Decisions can be done anywhere and at any time.

Colonel Dawson fought for me in 2010. As a result, I became battalion commander. There was pushback regarding my getting promoted until she said, "Harris is my guy." She told the General, "He works his fingers off and he spends 15 hours a day here. He is highly qualified and exceeds all the requirements. This is what is going to happen. I am the commander, and this is the guy I want." In many ways, she was just like Colonel Carl Pfeiffer, whom I'll tell you about in a subsequent chapter.

When You Recognize Good Leadership, Speak Up

One time there was a meeting and Colonel Dawson stepped out of the room to go to the restroom. All of a sudden the staff opened up and, there was all this discussion about this, that, and the other thing. I stood up (I was the senior officer in the room) and said, "Guys, this is the way this is going to go down. There's one person in charge and we all need to get on the same page so she can make good decisions—and, just as a reminder, everything is open to discussion until the boss makes a decision. Once the decision is made, so long as it is not illegal or immoral, we will as a staff figure out how to support and execute it." She came in while I was on my soapbox and everyone stood up. Then she proceeded to lead the group.

Later she said to me, "Dan, thanks for doing that. This is the level I need the staff to get to and I see that slowly happening."

Another time in Kuala Lumpur, Malaysia, we were conducting a combined civilian and military exercise involving humanitarian assistance disaster relief (HaDR) and redeploying a BCT to the Continental United States (CONUS). As the senior (U.S.) military commander on the ground, Colonel Dawson was asked in a CNN interview about the difficulty and frustration and bureaucracy of having to work with a mix of non-governmental organizations (NGOs) in the same battle space as the military. Without missing a beat, she replied that there was nothing to be frustrated about and that bureaucracy was a good thing that was put in place to slow down the process—to make it more deliberate and thoughtful. I thought the reply was brilliant and timely, especially when leading a force deployed in a foreign country and working with different countries' military and NGOs.

In addition to Malaysia, we ended up going on missions to Nicaragua, and Hokkaido, Japan. They all went off very well.

Because Colonel Stephanie Dawson led with integrity, I would follow her to the ends of the earth.

***

CHAPTER 21
Colonel Mark Moser

"Great leaders are almost always great simplifiers, who can cut through argument, debate, and doubt to offer a solution everyone can understand."—General Colin Powell

Another great leader I admired was Mark Moser. He was an active duty colonel who, along with another active duty colonel named Mike Hamlet, came into the Division G3 Plans section at Fort Drum. They introduced themselves as the new Chief(s) of Plans. Colonel Moser was an Army aviator, a PAC (rotary wing) helicopter pilot. I was a captain and worked as the G4 planner—the lead for writing the G4 Annex of the Division's Operations Order—from April to December 2004 (when we arrived in Kuwait).

When we crossed into Iraq, I was assigned as Iraqi Security Forces Resource Manager. Colonel Moser got a new assignment when we arrived in theater as well. In Tikrit, he was assigned as the Iraqi Security Forces (ISF) Cell Chief.

In theater, in Tikrit, there was the Iraqi Security Force (ISF) cell (I was in charge of doing the planning), the Iraqi Army (IA), and the Iraqi Police (IP), as well as the Iraqi Border Security Forces (IBSF). Colonel Moser liaised between the U.S. (the political end of the military) and the Iraqis. Everything we did was for the Iraqis. We pretty much planned, resourced and ran everything for the Iraqis. There were logisticians and intel personnel. I was in charge of logistics. Colonel Moser interfaced with division headquarters.

I enjoy military planning for its detail-oriented, multiple consideration operations on different levels. There was lots of research and cross-indexing involved. When a plan was developed, we needed to "wargame" the plan, then make adjustments and changes. Then we had to repeat the wargame with each section of the Blue Force and the Red Force countering each action. The Blue Force would develop solution sets to offset the Red Force's counter action.

If you enjoy planning as I do, this becomes fun. It is not work. The hours were long, and we worked six (and sometimes seven) days at a time. Even for work that you consider fun, if you don't take any breaks, the work will push you over the edge—especially since planners are in general detail-minded individuals who will examine and analyze the hair and color on a gnat's ass. The downside was that over time, the work environment became very stressful.

Just how stressful was demonstrated when a fight broke out between two majors, with one officer attempting to push another out the second-floor window of a World War II style barracks building at Drum. Thankfully he was not successful, and others separated them. But the atmosphere was quite intense all of the time.

Colonel Moser was an instructor at the School of Advanced Military Studies (SAMS), which we in the community called "Jedi Night School." It is a very selective military school of soldiers with advanced degrees. These were mostly a bunch of PhDs and PhD candidates. I looked forward to competing for a slot and Colonel Moser said he would recommend me for it.

Know How to Delegate

In response to the fight between the two majors, Colonel Moser called the entire team in and said these few words: "This deployment is a marathon and not a sprint. Therefore, pace yourselves or you will get burned out. When you burn out, you do stupid stuff—like fight. Remember, the enemy is not here. Instead, he is across the pond in theater. Don't forget that!" Colonel Moser was one of the leaders who taught me that it is not the many words that have the most meaning.

Following his talk to us, he instituted mandatory days off. He then charged the section NCO with drawing up plans for days on and rest days. Colonel Moser delegated extensively. Rarely did he ever get involved in the nuts-and-bolts kinds of issues, unless there was a disagreement that couldn't get resolved by the senior NCO (who was in charge of the shop and did all the grunt work).

Colonel Moser was memorable because of his leadership style. He was very direct. He had tons of courage and I respected him for that. He had a sense of humor and would joke around. But he was serious when he had to be. If he thought you were bullshitting, he threw down the BS flag and he'd call you on the carpet for it in a heartbeat. He was very competent, he cared, and everything was about doing the Army's work.

***

CHAPTER 22
Colonel Carl Pfeiffer

"Don't be the nut in the fruit cocktail." —Carl Pfeiffer

I also enjoyed working with Colonel Carl Pfeiffer. He was the 42nd Infantry Division Chief Personnel Officer (known as the G1) when I reported to the division for the deployment to Tikrit, Iraq, for Operation Iraqi Freedom 3 (although I would not meet Colonel Pfeiffer until the division arrived in Iraq). He remained the G1 throughout the deployment. Unlike many officers who either transitioned or rotated out of their position (in fact, the division changed the Chief of Staff twice while I was there), Colonel Pfeiffer never changed position.

History of the 42nd

The 42nd infantry was originally Douglas MacArthur's. Comprising National Guard troops from 26 states and the District of Columbia, the Chief of Staff of the newly created 42nd Division, Colonel Douglas MacArthur (he didn't become a general until WWII) remarked that the 42nd was truly a "national unit," with its component units stretching across the country from coast to coast, "like a rainbow." The name stuck and the 42nd became known as the Rainbow Division.

From its activation in August of 1917 through the Armistice in November 1918, the 42nd was in combat longer than any other American division and suffered greater than 50 percent casualties. To memorialize the half of the division's soldiers who had been killed or wounded during the war, Rainbow Division Soldiers modified the patch to a quarter arc, by cutting the symbol in half.

Out of the Three Gs—Grace, Generosity, and Gratitude—Grace is Colorblind

It is important to know history well so that you can always place the present in historical context, to guide your walk on the path forward. I worked in the Division headquarters in Troy, New York, home of Uncle Sam, for the famous 42nd Infantry Division. While there I was always reminded that there was once a controversy as to whether to combine the 42nd with the 369th. When the New York National Guardsmen of the 42nd Infantry Division (the Rainbow Division) left for the Great War, they were given a jubilant send-off. Another group of men also from New York, the all-black 369th, also left for the war but were not part of the parade—because those who opposed any send-off argued that "black was not a color of the rainbow." But their opponents, the German soldiers, would name them "Hellfighters."

Meeting Colonel Pfeiffer

Back in Tikrit, Iraq, while walking outside Saddam's palace enjoying the warm evening breeze from the Tigris River, I came across the O-6 Operations Colonel, Mario Castagliola, while he was on his smoke break. I knew Colonel "C" and I admired and respected him. He was an armor officer, but he was down to earth and very approachable.

We talked about family and the war, then he asked how I was holding up in the ISF. As we discussed the challenges of working logistics and operations with the Iraqi army, he asked me why I hadn't been promoted (I was a captain at the time). In his opinion, I was eligible: I exceeded all of the requirements, and was a team player and a hard worker. He told me, "Go see Colonel Pfeiffer tomorrow," and, "Do what he tells you to do." So I went to see Colonel Pfeiffer the next day.

Colonel Carl Pfeiffer was passionate about soldiers getting recognized for what they were worth. He was tall and big (he would've made a poor infantryman) and confident. He said, "Give me these six things and I'll work on your packet." A promotion packet is the collection of required documents needed to be considered for promotion.

So I went right back to my hooch (bunk), got the documents and brought them to him. He was impressed. He said, "I'll get back to you." Then he said, "Wait a second. You had those documents with you?" I replied that I had them in my survival pack, which I store with my belongings. I always packed three bags, one of which is my survival pack. If I had to move in a hurry and could not take anything else, I would take my survival pack. It was small, waterproof, and lightweight. Few things qualified to be in the survival pack, and my record is one. In peacetime, I kept paper copies. But in theater, I don't need paper copies, so it's easier to carry them on a CD and backup thumb drive.

I didn't realize at the time that this interaction would be my saving grace less than a year later.

Eight months or so went by, and he was getting bombarded with requests from all these soldiers (he was a very popular man). Even senior non-commissioned officers (NCOs) would be after him. He said in a meeting jokingly, "You colonels are always bugging me. There's a captain who has never asked me about his promotion. Why aren't you all like Harris? Harris, why aren't you pestering me like these other guys?"

I said, "Sir, you are a full bird colonel in the United States Army and that is all that I need to know. You said you would get back to me and I trust that you will." Once again, Colonel Pfeiffer was impressed.

When the deployment was over and we landed at the Rapid Deployment Facility (RDF) at Fort Drum, New York, he was getting off the plane and was informed that I was going to be assigned to work in Buffalo, New York, on a full-time basis. I learned later that he told some of his people, "That is a seven-hour drive away from Harris's family in good weather. That doesn't make sense." He was rotating to become the chief of staff at the Division. "Let me talk to him," he insisted. So he spoke with me and came up with a plan.

He said, "You come to work in Troy for me in Logistics. You can come in Monday morning at 1100 hours—later than the others, after you see your kids off to school—and then leave at 1300 early Friday afternoon. That way you can eat dinner with your kids and be with your family on the weekends." I was commuting from Northeast Pennsylvania, which was three to four hours away from Troy, New York. "I've seen you work," he said. "Work is not an issue for you. You will be clocking in 15- to 17-hour workdays anyway." So I got quarters to live at Watervliet, New York (the place that made cannons in the Civil War). This was palatable for my family and it was important to them. They felt that this senior officer named Colonel Pfeiffer cared about them personally—although I cannot say the same about many other senior officers.

I liked him because he went to the mat, not only for me, but for many soldiers. And he threw out the BS flag in a heartbeat. He did not like long explanations and he was quick to cut to the chase and separate the fluff from the bottom line. When you dealt with him, you always knew to be prepared. He despised incompetent and selfish leaders and would say leaders need to be competent, selfless, and fair.

I began to learn how to be an effective staff officer under his tutelage. I said to myself, "I want to be like this guy." He held weekly staff meetings on Mondays at 0900. It was a three-hour drive but I wanted to be there for them, so I made them. I wasn't going to let him down.

Colonel Carl Pfeiffer reinforced in me the attitude that "you fight for your people." Those things stayed with me.

Specialist Cobb

Another instance of Colonel Pfeiffer's leadership dealt with a good friend of mine, Andre Cobb. Specialist Cobb was an E-4. There were senior officers and NCOs sitting in his office conference room when Colonel Pfeiffer said to the sergeant major, "I want Cobb's promotion. I've got no movement on it for a while." Cobb was one of three young African-American full-time soldiers working in the division headquarters.

He noticed that the promotions went to the white soldiers in a timely manner—while for others it was very slow. As a former G1 personnel officer, he knew the process. He said, "I see what's going on around here. Anybody that doesn't is kidding themselves."

As a leader, you always need to see and hear everything that's going on. You see first, hear first. Colonel Pfeiffer would say, "Pay attention. Point out the nut that is in the fruit cocktail." You don't necessarily need to do and say something about everything, but you need to recognize it. Colonel Pfeiffer saw the disparity in quantity, ranks and qualifications between blacks and whites. The result was that Cobb was promoted!

Major General Garrett

Another example of a leader who lived by the nut in the fruit cocktail analogy in Troy was Major General George Garrett, the Commanding General (CG). I remember from the late 1990s a senior staff meeting of colonels from the states that made up the division. The CG walked in and we all stood up and he greeted us and told us to sit down. As a first lieutenant, I was there to set up chairs and tables, distribute file documents and take notes. He looked around the drill floor in Troy and asked, "Where are my minority officers in this division? I mean, this is the Rainbow Division, isn't it?" He went on to say, "All I see before me in this room are a bunch of old, bald-headed white men, so I ask you 'Where are the minority officers in this Rainbow Division?'"

The place became deadly silent. From my vantage point—seated in the corner with my poster size paper-boards for note taking—I could see the entire room. I saw that other than me, there was one other person of color, a Hispanic officer (both of us very low-ranking), present. The CG then gave out a stunning assignment to his colonels. He tasked them with bringing with them, to the next year's assembly of colonels, the profile information of a minority officer that they were mentoring and coaching. He said that they would tell him the officer's name, spouse's name, children's names, and where they lived. He also wanted to know what their profession was and what their aspirations were. And, more importantly, the colonels had to tell him how they would help these officers to achieve their goals in their units.

I was not present for the next meeting of colonels in Troy. But the nut in the fruit cocktail had been called out. And indeed, grace is colorblind.

Students of Pfeiffer

A few other officers and soldiers started calling ourselves the "Students of Pfeiffer." Many of us asked him to be our mentor. We were all majors by then.

We admired him. It was because, internally, we all knew he was very selfless and he was reasonable. He wouldn't ask us to do anything he wouldn't do himself, even when it came down to doing push-ups, sit-ups, or running. He wasn't sitting in his office like 90 percent of the other senior officers. He was about doing the Army's business. He was candid, even though others (particularly other senior officers) didn't care for—or appreciate—his leadership style.

He knew his business and he fought for his people. Whenever he said, "I want this done," we delivered for him. If you didn't deliver the first time, he would call you out, but not in a derogatory way. You didn't feel humiliated when he did, but he had no tolerance for incompetence. Because of that, the next time you went in to see him, your "t's" were crossed and your "i's" were dotted.

***

CHAPTER 23
Colonel Dave Cox

"True humility is not thinking less of yourself; it is thinking of yourself less." —Rick Warren

Colonel Dave Cox was my boss when I worked in the Joint Action Control Office (JACO) at the Pentagon in 2015. He was in the Air Force. He taught me how to think strategically—or as the 38th Chief of Staff of the Army, General Raymond Odierno, used to put it: "I want officers who can think a mile wide and one inch deep."

Officers need to make decisions and to do so effectively. You need to think from a high-level, birds-eye view to be able to connect the dots. After I met Colonel Cox, I saw in practice what I had heard and learned about—that each service: Army, Air Force, Navy, Marines, and Coast Guard—all think differently and each has its own culture and language. Of the Army, Air Force, Navy, Coast Guard, and the Marines, the Army understandably (as well as the Marines to some extent) has a "boots on the ground" mentality. They fight on the terrain. They could tough out just about any situation imaginable.

The Air Force guys, like Colonel Cox, are different, with a particular culture and language. They fight in the air. They are usually fighter pilots or transport pilots and support staff. They have a broader, more strategic perspective on what is happening.

Colonel Cox dealt with the Joint Staff, which includes the Office of the Secretary of Defense (OSD). The Secretary of Defense (SecDef) is the leader and chief executive officer of the United States Department of Defense. He leads the executive department of the Armed Forces of the U.S. and is a civilian. He consults with the president. Colonel Cox was an F-16 fighter pilot, now doing his office time. He got me to learn and understand many different things at a very high, strategic DoD level.

Policy Writing

One time, there was a change I wanted to make in how things were being done and I spoke with him. He had me put together a policy memorandum that would impact the 450,000 service members of the Army National Guard. I needed to "staff action" the memo, meaning I had to coordinate and collaborate with relevant stakeholders and finally get it through the legal office before presenting it to the General for approval and signing.

I put it together and he read it and laughed. He looked at me and tore it up. He said, "That would be great for a battalion of 1,400 soldiers, but I need you to think policy level."

He wanted me to think at the 90,000-foot level, a mile wide but only one inch deep. This memo had to change behavior as well as change thinking. It had to be forceful enough to change the way its readers would do something, stipulating how I wanted them to do it. He wanted me to think strategically, "big picture."

At the time, I was the Chief of the Executive Secretariat's office. The Executive Secretariat is all about coordination and collaboration of relevant items. There are more than 400,000 National Guardsmen and women in the United States. There are issues that the National Guard Joint Staff, including the Executive Secretariat, has to deal with. We would hear from citizens, senators, congressmen and congresswomen, as well as agencies such as the Department of Justice, the Department of State, and the Chief of Staff. We received and staffed actions from Senator John McCain a lot, usually with a short turnaround time to respond.

This type of correspondence would come through my office. The team would do the research and begin the coordination process to determine who needed to have a voice in the matter; we wanted to identify all relevant stakeholders to elicit their input. We received all the stakeholders' input, generated the document while capturing the chief's voice, and sent it through legal. This was all done before it got up to the four star-level for approval and signature.

As chief, I provided oversight on quality control and worked to mitigate redo. You never wanted the chief to return your staff action for a redo. It meant that your staff did a poor job, and that reflects on you. The objective was to anticipate and do great staff work.

Humility Can Be a Learned Skill

Colonel Cox was humble and a very, very smart man. There was a warmth to him. He was also a man of faith. When my mother passed away, he wasn't at work that day. I left early (it can take anywhere from 20-30 minutes to get in and out of the Pentagon with all the security). Anyway, after he got the message, he called me in the evening and said, "Brother, if I were standing in front of you, I would kneel down and pray with you. I am so sorry for your loss."

That really touched me. He exhibited the pillar of love at a very vulnerable time for me.

When Colonel Cox retired, I told his mother about his response to me when my mother died. Her eyes kind of welled up and then she said, "You know, Dave has always been like that." I knew Colonel Cox was a man of faith because we talked about our faith every now and then, when time allowed.

He is someone I will always remember very warmly as he led with love.

***

CHAPTER 24
General Timothy McKeithen

"A man only learns by two things; one is reading and the other is association with smarter people." —Will Rogers

General Tim McKeithen was a two-star general and Deputy of the National Guard Bureau when I met him. He is African-American and a very strong-willed individual. He had a presence, even though he was of relatively small stature. He consistently maxed out the Army physical fitness test consisting of push-ups, sit-ups, and a two-mile run and was in great physical condition.

On the few occasions I was fortunate enough to interact with him, I felt like I was moving and thinking in slow motion only because he thought and moved so quickly. He had a positive and strong attitude.

Just how much he was admired was driven home to me one day before the start of a meeting with a group of general officers (GOs)—officers who had achieved at least the rank of one-star general. The chance to work with GOs is one of the great opportunities that comes from working in the Pentagon. GOs are not dummies. At the GO level, you clearly have to have some gray matter between your ears. While there, I would listen and thereby learn how to *think* from these individuals. I always appreciated learning.

On that day, a group of general officers were sitting around talking as they waited for the meeting to start, and one of them said, "You know, McKeithen always thinks he's the smartest guy in the room." And they all laughed. Then there was a pregnant pause and another one piped up, "Actually, here's the scary part. He usually IS the smartest guy in the room." There was more laughter, mostly because they knew it was true.

I was laughing inside. My boss told me I could leave the room. I always practiced protocol with senior leaders and only "broke contact" when I was dismissed. I chuckled as I left the room.

Wisdom

I came to the U.S. from Liberia when I was 15 years old. My grandfather, Pedro, said to my brother and me, "Always cherish knowledge. Pursue knowledge like it is the most beautiful woman you have ever seen in your life. You've got to have her. You're not going to stop until you get her." He continued, "I don't know where you boys will end up, or whether I'll ever see you again… but in this book lies all the answers to all the questions you're ever going to have in life. I don't have gold or silver to give you, but I do have this book. Make sure that you keep it with you and read it." It was his Bible.

Remembering the words of my grandfather, I always had a fondness for learning. I would try to be like a sponge. My business was the military. It is both an art and a craft. I studied the military, thought about it, and strove to learn all I could about it by availing myself of military people who were at the top of their game. Like knowledge and a verbal conversation with God, you can never achieve it, you can only get close to it. Anyway, I liked being around general officers like Tim McKeithen. They're very bright folks.

I was often part of classified-level discussions. The discussions would frequently center on or around North Korea or Russia and other heavy topics like that. Once meetings were over, you could kind of feel the air thin out a little bit and people would turn their attention to simple discussions and casual conversations.

Getting Called Up

General McKeithen called me one time when I was still in command with the 369th Hellfighters (before I went to work at the Guard Bureau in Arlington, Virginia). I don't know where he got my information, but somehow he knew I was going to work at the Bureau.

Anyway, Captain JC Bravo came running into my office and said, "General McKeithen's aide is on the phone and the General wants to speak to you." This was the first time I spoke with him and he told me there were things that I needed to know when I arrived, so I could "navigate the walls of the Bureau smoothly." What he meant by this was there were certain people, places, conversations to avoid, so I didn't get myself into a quagmire. So he suggested I make a note and get in touch with him when I arrived. (Conversations with the General were always very short and direct: 30 seconds to a minute. If you found yourself talking with him for five minutes or longer, it was either something very bad or something very good).

Seven months or so later, when I got to Arlington, he had been reassigned as deputy to the United States Northern Command (NORTHCOM), and so we never had the follow-up conversation—although I saw him in the halls of the Pentagon a few times.

I did have another one-on-one with General McKeithen when I had an opportunity to go before the Department of Army Board for O-6 Colonel. He told me the review board would spend less than two minutes to review my packet application because there were lieutenant colonels from all over the country who were eligible and trying to get promoted. He wanted to go over a few things with me, so when I went in front of the board, I'd be successful.

The packet itself is your army record of all of your work assignments and your performance in those assignments along with your potential as deemed by your rater, usually a senior leader. It also deals with such things as your education/schooling, your physical fitness (which had to be in good order), your awards, your annual evaluations, things like that. If there was anything that raised an eyebrow, they would go on to the next applicant. If you were rejected, you would get a letter from the Department of the Army (DA) saying you didn't meet the requirements. You would get a second opportunity the following year to present your packet again to the board. And if you applied twice and weren't accepted after the second try, you automatically got dismissed from the Army with no appeals.

My Wake-Up Call

General McKeithen asked me to send him my packet and gave me the nuances that I needed to know. He surprised me with a comment he made after looking over my materials. He said if he were sitting on my board (which is typically a board of GOs because they'd be selecting colonels), "On a scale of one to five, with one being bad and five being great, I would give you a two!" Ouch!

He basically told me my packet was screwed up. He pointed out that my evaluations were poorly written. He told me I should have questioned the way the evaluations were put together. "Don't just read it and take it as, 'This is it,'" he advised. We had a quick discussion. He gave me some things to fix. Things you want to have in your evaluations, he said, included wording such as, "He led," "He directed," or "He developed," when writing about your performance for the period. And phrases like, "has the potential to excel and perform at a higher level" would go a long way toward receiving serious consideration.

Dreams Do Come True

Anyway, I submitted my packet in 2017 and I was cleared for promotion on the first try. I was eligible to be promoted to a full-bird colonel! I got my DA letter. I had met the selection criteria. I had become worthy of being promoted to Eagle!

Trust me, it is a big deal to get that letter. I attribute that success 100 percent to General McKeithen.

The downside when this happens, however, is you need the state or the Army or the boss to back you. Your boss has to give you a shot. When I was in Arlington, my boss kept saying, "Continue, continue. You're doing a great job there."

The subsequent conversation with my boss in New York was like a shotgun blast to my chest. Back in October 2013, after three years in Battalion Command with excellent evaluations, his only phone call to me was, "I have given out all the jobs and I don't have a job for your follow-on, so you will go and work at the Bureau until something opens up." In September 2016, his other phone call to me was, "You need to return to New York and finish out your last two years in Counter Drug, then retire. We don't owe you anything."

He was a two-star general and I was only a lieutenant colonel. So that was that.

My friends would say to me, "All you have to do is wait for an O-6 slot." But the reality was, there wasn't a slot. Besides, I would have had to go through a guy who didn't want me.

Onward and Upward

I decided not to fight it or ask for assistance from other GOs because everything had to go through him. The Lord has always guided me. I left it up to God and my faith. If I'd pinned on O-6, I could have worked in the army until 2021, three additional years.

When I went on active duty, my goal was to become a general officer. I wanted to become a GO because I wanted to be a decision-maker at the highest levels, to develop the policies, plans and strategies being discussed for the year 2050—and beyond. I wanted to participate and have a say in what our great military will look like and how we will fight and win America's wars in 30 to 50 years.

But now, I have other ambitions. Leadership is about being flexible, adaptable, re-inventing yourself and redefining your goals and ambitions—either for yourself or your organization. I would say that General McKeithen embodied all four pillars: courage, love, integrity, and passion.

***

PART 5

CRISIS LEADERSHIP

In 1957, The National Guard was called on by Arkansas Governor Orval Faubus to "preserve the peace" when nine black students tried to integrate Central High School in Little Rock. Shortly thereafter, President Dwight D. Eisenhower federalized that same Guard and ordered them (along with the U.S. Army's 101st Airborne Division) to integrate the school. In the sixties, President John F. Kennedy sent the Guard to Birmingham to oversee the integration of the University of Alabama and that state's public school (much to the dismay of Governor George Wallace). And, after Martin Luther King, Jr. was assassinated, President Lyndon B. Johnson ordered National Guard units to quell riots in Chicago, Baltimore, and Washington, D.C.

The National Guard has 343,000 soldiers, eight division headquarters, 27 combat teams, 55 functional brigades, 42 multifunctional brigades, eight combat aviation brigades and two Special Forces groups. It is an integral part of the U.S. armed forces. Today it operates 42 percent of all military aircraft and supplies.

Another unique feature of the Guard is the Chief of the National Guard Bureau, a four-star billet, whom I worked for as his Executive Secretariat in the Joint Action Control Office (JACO) and part of the Joint Staff. The position interfaces with more than 27 federal agencies such as the Department of Homeland Security (DHS) and FEMA, the Department of State, all of the legislative members, all of the state governors, all of the combatant commanders as well as the president directly—unlike the other service chiefs such as the heads of the Navy, Air Force, Army, and Marine Corps.

Members of the National Guard go everywhere the regular Army and Air Force goes. Guardsmen and women are now deployed in over 55 countries around the world, and with the Guard State Partnership Program (SPP), each state sponsors and partners with a foreign country where Guard men and women leverage their civilian expertise and military training to assist partner countries to train for and respond to natural disasters, policing, search and rescue, and so forth. Guard soldiers are appropriately suited for this role because they are civilians who live and work in their communities and, when called upon, can deploy and work with partner countries using their civilian experiences and leadership perspectives.

Members of the Guard are the evolution of the original states' militias, created for military purposes. Their core missions are threefold: fighting America's wars, securing the homeland, and building enduring partnerships. After 9.11 escalated the war on terror, these three things became of utmost importance.

The remainder of this book chronicles instances of stateside crises where the Guard was mobilized.

CHAPTER 25
Katrina and the Waves

"The road to success is always under construction."—Lily Tomlin

By many accounts, while the 9.11 terrorist attack was the worst man-made disaster to hit the United States, Hurricane Katrina was the worst natural disaster to hit the nation. Both left our country and our people with a big black eye. Both would require very strong leadership from elected officials, our National Guard, and thousands of ordinary people rising to the occasion to do extraordinary things in saving lives and property. These were everyday people who became inspired to do great things.

The death toll from Katrina is still not known. Some say it was 1,800 while others say it was closer to 3,500. The aftermath of both events needed leadership—to confidently reassure the people that, "We will be alright," to frame and communicate a vision for the way forward, and finally, to execute that vision with vigor and energy.

Hurricane Katrina decimated not only New Orleans, but also Slidell, Louisiana and Waveland and Biloxi, Mississippi. In addition, Mobile, Alabama had to deal with 10 feet of water.

A Parable

A story is told of a preacher who was on his roof during a storm similar to Katrina. One of the townsfolk went by in a canoe and said, "Get in!" The preacher said, "No, I'll be okay. I have faith in the Lord."

The next day, when the waters had risen higher, a first responder came by in a motorboat and said, "We need to get you out of here. The levee's going to break." The preacher replied, "I shall remain. The Lord will see me through."

The third day a helicopter flew overhead and a state trooper called down to him with a megaphone, "Grab the rope! This is your last chance." The preacher, steadfast in his beliefs, responded, "The Lord will deliver me."

Predictably, he drowns. He goes to heaven and gets an audience with the Lord. The preacher said, "Lord, I had unwavering faith in you. Why didn't you save me?"

The Lord replied, "What do you want from me? I sent you a canoe, a boat, and a helicopter."

Many Were in Denial

There is no arguing that some people were apathetic about the dire evacuation warnings that were given before Katrina made landfall. Two nights before its arrival, Bourbon Street was rocking with revelers partying well into the night.

President Bush declared a pre-hurricane state of emergency. Mayor Ray Nagin announced a mandatory evacuation. People were told repeatedly to get out and to get out as quickly as possible.

Unfortunately, more than one quarter of New Orleans' population live below the poverty level. Many of them didn't have the means to get out—or decided to ride it out. And there is an inherent bias against forcing people out of their own homes. Later, the painful lessons learned were not going to be wasted by Governor of Florida Rick Scott and Governor of Puerto Rico Ricardo Rossello for Hurricanes Michael and Maria, when they each ordered forced evacuation of citizens out of harm's way. Reflective leaders often make effective leadership decisions. I submit it is not a coincidence: reflection and effectiveness are related.

Plenty of Blame to Go Around

There is no doubt that mistakes were made in the aftermath of Katrina. On top of that, things got politicized. Before we get into that, however, let's look at the topography of the area.

The Mississippi River Delta is where the Mississippi River flows into the Gulf of Mexico. The major cities in that area include New Orleans, Louisiana and Biloxi, Mississippi. New Orleans is almost completely surrounded by water, with Lake Pontchartrain to the north and the Gulf of Mexico to the south. Most of the city is either at or 10 feet below sea level. On average, its streets are six feet below the gulf.

Geologically, the city is sinking. The soil there is naturally soft, wet, and spongy. Geologists use the word "subsidence" to describe the gradual caving in of land, which is the case there. It is estimated that they lose four feet every century. In that sense, a cataclysmic event of Katrina's magnitude was a disaster waiting to happen.

What Did Happen

Katrina made landfall as a Category 3 hurricane. The eye moved east and north of the city. However, the sigh of relief was short-lived. Because of its counter-clockwise motion, the hurricane picked up water from both Lake Pontchartrain and the Gulf of Mexico and directed it toward the city. This created a 15-foot storm surge.

The water from Lake Pontchartrain broke through one of the levees and water rushed into the city. Then another (the 17th Street) levee collapsed. And a third levee, London Street, broke.

The 350 miles of levees in the city were built many years prior to protect the land. In 1927, the U.S. Army Corp of Engineers took control of the levee system. The reality is they were slowly sinking and in need of repair. On top of that, they were built to contain only a Category 3 fast-moving storm. Katrina had escalated to a Category 5 with 155-plus mile-per-hour winds.

Backup System

The second line of defense was the pumping system. There were 24 water pumping stations capable of pumping 30 billion gallons of water a day. The pumps were inundated with floodwaters because of the levee breach. What would've taken about 12-20 hours, had the pumps and the levees done their jobs, instead took 21 grueling days. They had to shut down the pumps because the motors were exposed. The controls were under water—and water and electricity don't mix.

Then yet another engineering disaster happened. Despite an evacuation of biblical proportions, thousands of victims were left stranded. Up to 25,000 residents remained in the city. Many went to the Superdome.

The Superdome, the "shelter of last resort," had a huge part of its roof torn off. One of the exhaust dampers at the very top blew away as a result of the gale force winds. After that, 15-foot sections of the roof started peeling off. Nobody knew if the building was going to hold.

Conditions inside the building deteriorated rapidly. Rain pouring in shorted out the electrical system. They had to depend on a backup generator, which produced only limited lighting. After that, it was just a matter of time before they lost water pressure, so the toilets overflowed. It was reported that the smell was a cross between a garbage dump and a junkyard. Conditions resembled a third-world country.

Any Relief in Sight?

All of these engineering disasters coalesced and made matters worse. In many ways it was the perfect storm.

As a result of the massive storm surge, the bridge over Lake Pontchartrain leading to Route 10 collapsed. It was later reported that 435 segments of the concrete passage were damaged by the water pressure from underneath. Because the bridge fell like a domino, getting relief in the form of bottled water, flashlights, and food was challenging. People wanted to help but getting there was next to impossible. People with boats wanted to lend a hand and even that became overwhelming, too.

By now, tens of thousands of people had taken up residence in the Superdome and the convention center. It soon became evident that the Superdome was not a hospital. Nor was it a hotel. It was designed to house people for about four hours, not four days. There was no air conditioning in the Superdome and the heat and humidity was getting to people. And there was no food or water at the convention center.

The Aftermath

The bottom line is the Gulf Coast lost its battle with Katrina. On top of that, there was looting and robbery. There were even accusations of stabbings, murder, and gang rape. The only thing that remained was the finger-pointing.

When you are standing at the edge of the world and it is going to hell in a handbasket, any idiot can see that there is a problem. The genius is in being able to surmise that there will be a problem days, months, even years before.

Poor leaders indulge in finger-pointing. It masks and detracts from their lack of planning and effective decision-making. Good leaders do not engage in it. They see it as distracting, and it shifts energy and time away from their focus and the issue at hand. Personally, I despise it because it is a complete waste of time and energy.

***

CHAPTER 26
True Grit

"The first responsibility of a leader is to define reality. The last is to say thank you. In between, the leader is a servant."—Max de Pree

As the world watched, America seemed to be bumbling and tripping over itself in knowing how to fix the problem. I submit to you that the missing piece was simply a leader.

From that standpoint, Katrina was hardly an inspiring performance by New Orleans Mayor Ray Nagin and Louisiana Governor Kathleen Blanco, especially in a post-9.11 world. When you compare and contrast them to New York City Mayor Rudy Giuliani and New York State Governor George Pataki, their collaboration left much to be desired. Despite that it happened less than four years after the terrorist attack on our homeland, nearly everyone was woefully ill-prepared for a disaster of this magnitude. These two individuals were no exception.

Yes, just when you thought the tragedy couldn't get any worse, politics entered the picture. Unlike in the aftermath of September 11, 2001, when Giuliani, Pataki, and Bush cooperated, Nagin, Blanco, and (the very same) Bush didn't. It was reported that Governor Blanco refused President Bush's offer to take over the National Guard. And the Federal Emergency Management Agency (FEMA) had recently been demoted (it was now part of the Department of Homeland Security and no longer fell under the authority of the president). Obviously, this didn't help matters.

One Person Can Make a Difference

There seemed to be no plan, no order, and no cohesion. While politicians pontificated, posed, and pointed, Lieutenant General Russel

L. Honoré was called to the scene. He had been ordered to coordinate all active-duty troops from every military branch for rescue, recovery, and security.

A native of nearby Lakeland, Louisiana, Honoré describes himself as an "African-American Creole," a combination that includes French, African-American, Indian, and Spanish ancestry. Others called him "The Ragin' Cajun." But to the sick, suffering, and needy in New Orleans, he became known simply as "that John Wayne dude who's getting things done." He would soon be tagged with another moniker: "The Category 5 General."

A leader needs to be aware of the optics of the situation he finds himself in and go to work to shape it daily. He needs to be aware that his credibility as a leader comes from the people or the team he is leading. Clearly in the case of The Ragin' Cajun, the people perceived him to be a more effective leader than the governor, mayor, and president combined—even though it was the president who sent him to Louisiana to work the issue.

A Farmer

Prior to his command of Joint Task Force Katrina, Lieutenant General Honoré went on numerous tours of duty that included Germany and South Korea. He saw action in Iraq and Kuwait during Operation Desert Storm. He also served in a variety of command and staff positions which focused on defense support to civil authorities and homeland defense. He supported the Department of Defense planning and response for Hurricanes Floyd in 1999; Isabel in 2003; and Charley, Frances, Ivan, and Jeanne in 2004. In addition, "Russ" also held a master's degree in human resource management when he arrived in Katrina's aftermath.

Some people believe image is everything. He had that covered with the swagger, the ever-present stogie, the heft and the height of his physique. He had the caramel skin, a 6'2" frame and a pencil mustache. For those not caught up in appearances, he was a soldier's soldier, a no-nonsense guy—the kind of man you want in the trenches with you.

His philosophy was, "It takes a big personality to command the army east of the Mississippi River." Legend has it that he was born in a hurricane. He went to school for agriculture but got caught up in the military. Honoré graduated from Southern University and A&M College in Baton Rouge. One of 12 children, including a line of eight boys, he was the youngest. After college, he worked on a dairy farm that grew sugar cane, cotton, and corn. They also had pigs and cows. Known in Atlanta for the vegetable garden he maintained outside his home there, he harvested potatoes, peppers, okra, and corn.

Deeds, Not Words

In the initial aftermath of a catastrophic event, the leader need not ponder and think, but do. It needs to be controlled, but it does not need to be refined: just do something. Without the advantage of deliberate and well-thought analysis, the leader needs to leverage gut instinct and just do something. They need to be open to entertaining and discussing the merits of their actions when the situation calms down, but now there is only one thing—and that is to do something—to alleviate pain and suffering, and save life, eyesight, and limbs.

Unfortunately, the opposite is exactly what was happening in Katrina—until Honoré arrived on the scene. The first tenet of leadership is, "Be present now, now be present," and the General performed this by exercising critical time and place. Every leader must quickly find that and place himself there to act as a catalyst to drive in the desired direction. Otherwise, the action will fail.

During World War II, General Doolittle recognized this and ordered that his bomber aircraft be moved from the back of the line to the front of the line on the aircraft carrier, giving himself the shortest runway possible for take-off to conduct the Tokyo Raid. This action not only bolstered the confidence of the other bomber pilots in their leader, it also assured them that they would be able to take off.

In another example of critical time and place, General Eisenhower visited his men in the 101st Airborne to simply smoke a cigarette and chat—to demonstrate his appreciation and understanding of what they were about to do in their assignment to parachute behind enemy lines and slow down Nazi armor and reinforcements to the beaches on D-Day. They were basically going on a suicide mission. The 101st sustained over eighty percent casualties.

First Stop

During Katrina, General Honoré's first stop was the Superdome. There he was seen discussing and executing a vision, a plan. This is what the people experienced and this is what they came to respect. He called Katrina a "worthy adversary" and spoke of her in military terms. He said she used a "classic military operation," one of overwhelming force. She even cut her enemy's ability to communicate. Essentially, she took her "enemy's eyes ... and ears out," he explained. In his estimation, Katrina fixed her opponent so he couldn't maneuver.

Creativity and Boldness

I remember watching a news video clip in which General Honoré told Louisiana National Guard soldiers, "Hey there, put away that weapon. You are here to assist these people...." as his Humvee drove by on his way to his headquarters as the commander of Joint Task Force Katrina.

When people have been traumatized and are in disbelief from the devastation that happened to them, they don't need to see American soldiers with weapons in their hands on the streets. We have civilian police agencies for that.

Instead, they need to see a show of force, discipline, and the "can do" attitude that soldiers are known for. The General knew that as a matter of fact. The leader must always balance the mindset and perception of the people in relation to the response you plan to apply to their problem. You do not have free will to conduct business unchecked.

I appreciated the General's focused and direct approach to problem-solving, using his "Don't get stuck on stupid" philosophy. Because, if left unchecked, minor problems could become major issues. By the time any situation involves and requires input from a leader, that leader needs to operate outside the known rules to effectively resolve the issue. This is especially why the leader is needed: to use creativity and boldness.

Honoré collaborated with other leaders on the USS Iwo Jima, which was anchored on the Mississippi River in New Orleans, to alleviate the suffering of the people dealing with this unprecedented disaster. Here was the first official on the scene who seemed to be taking charge.

***

CHAPTER 27
Lessons Learned from Katrina

"First, break all the rules." —Marcus Buckingham

After Katrina hit, there was untold suffering. Some died after being displaced. Flooding left 80 percent of New Orleans under water. The barrier islands had done little to protect the mainland as they got hammered, too.

The National Guard

Soon after General Honoré assumed command, the natural disaster turned man-made disaster was finally getting the leadership it needed. The National Guard began to retake the city. A half-million Guard troops were mobilized for the search-and-rescue mission. They went door-to-door looking for survivors. The Louisiana National Guard marched into the Convention Center, and within 30 minutes they restored order and began to distribute food and water. Within 36 hours, they evacuated 25,000 people from the building. Those people were bused and flown to shelters around the country, primarily Houston and Atlanta. Finally, there was movement.

The Guard, in tandem with FEMA, did all they could to rescue the "bitter enders." A number of boats arrived. The boats and helicopters were the only way to help out initially, as the airport was closed—and so was access from Interstate 10. Numerous pilots of Coast Guard and National Guard helicopters acted heroically to pluck people off rooftops and bring them to safety. At long last, it seemed that Americans were helping Americans.

This scene would be repeated again and again as people helped people in Superstorm Sandy and Hurricane Maria. This is the same spirit that embodied the earlier settlers of the Massachusetts Bay Colony, the minutemen, who dropped everything they were doing to respond to the emergency at hand in order to support their fellow citizens. Given good leadership and resources, people can handle any disaster they face, provided they utilize courage, love, integrity, and passion. Honoré used all four pillars to perfection.

Paradigm Shift

People were grateful for General Honoré and his leadership. Congress ultimately passed a $10.5 billion bill for disaster aid. And to think that much of this could have been prevented, if only a) the infrastructure had been kept up, b) the elected leaders had done their part, and c) people had listened to the warning signs to evacuate to safety.

Many people today insist that Hurricane Katrina was the beginning of the end for President George W. Bush. It was stated that "he doesn't care about black people." Whether true or not, the appearance became the reality. Optics are always important. I firmly believe that this unnatural human catastrophe—and the leadership void that occurred at the top—went a long way toward ushering in the Obama era.

Leaders need to be aware that people don't care that you did great and wonderful things four years prior, during 9.11. The people only care about what you can deliver for them now. It will be worthwhile to remember to always be present now, and practice critical time and place.

The effectiveness of the Guard is its ability to take the principles of war and elements of battle and leverage them against catastrophic civilian events to arrive at a solution in a civilian setting. Likewise, the Guard also has the ability to flex and leverage civilian experiences, and civilian agencies' best practices and lessons learned from combat battlefield situations in the military contemporary operating environment.

I have witnessed this taking place repeatedly.

Breaking the Rules

As the national leader of our country, President Bush had strong leaders who did not operate with a rule book in Governor Pataki and Mayor Giuliani, while, in the case of Katrina, he did not have the same in Blanco and Nagin. For those of us who remembered what happened, this is a classic case of compare and contrast in basic leadership. Regrettably, we would later repeat the same mistakes for another monster hurricane called Maria when it came to Florida and the territory of Puerto Rico.

Tools of the Trade

Just as leaders need to know when to break the rules to bring about a resolution, leaders also need to know how to apply just the right type of tool and the right amount of pressure. Leaders always need to maintain a diversified leadership kit bag and need to be skillful and resourceful enough to know what type of tool to use for a given situation. Not every problem requires a heavy hand with a bat or gentle persuasion. While some problems require a sledgehammer to get a resolution, another problem might only require a gentle tap. The effective leader needs to know which to use and what time to use it. The decision is theirs alone.

When tragedy strikes, effective leaders rise to the occasion and make good decisions only if they are prepared to break the rules and use their diversified leadership kit bag. They need to appropriately use the right tool and apply the right amount of pressure to achieve resolution. Good leaders understand this role is one of honor and they need to respect the people they come to lead and serve. When you arrive to help and lead people, you are not given carte blanche to lead unchecked.

Thus, according to General Honoré, "Effective leadership involves breaking the rules." You don't ring the doorbell to get access to a burning house. Instead, you violently break down the windows or doors so that you can search and rescue—in order to save the lives of its inhabitants. Leaders exist to make decisions when the moment requires it and nothing else. Mayor Rudy Giuliani, Governor George Pataki, and LTG Russel Honoré all knew this when their moment came. They each employed courage, love, integrity, and passion.

***

CHAPTER 28
The Perfect Storm

"We cannot stop natural disasters but we can arm ourselves with knowledge; so many lives wouldn't have to be lost if there was enough disaster preparedness."—Petra Nemcova

Hurricane Sandy was a 21st-century storm. It was a hybrid—two storms in one. I've heard it said that it was the equivalent of five Hiroshima bombs. Well, however you want to describe it, it was a storm of epic proportions.

Hurricane or Superstorm?

As I understand it, the difference between a hurricane and a superstorm is that a superstorm often refers to cold, non-tropical weather, while a hurricane feeds off of warm, tropical weather conditions. A hurricane has a calm eye, with warm water present on all sides—and a spiraling band.

Apparently, Sandy was a hurricane as it moved up the coast and then became a superstorm as it encountered colder water. It was then that it took on the makeup of a more traditional winter-style storm. Because it came around Halloween, it was coined (by Jim Cisco, a forecaster at the Hydrometeorological Prediction Center), "Frankenstorm Sandy."

CNN banned the use of the moniker, "Frankenstorm," saying it trivialized the destruction. Some also feel the term "superstorm" causes confusion—that the definition doesn't do it justice. Regardless, it cost nearly $70 billion in damage, despite its moving inland and losing strength. If you were in the line of it, as many Americans were, the nomenclature is irrelevant.

Nature Took Things Back

When Henry Hudson arrived in Manhattan 400 years ago, there were bears in Central Park. Wolves howled atop hills in midtown. Fish swam in streams that snaked their way through the Financial District.

Manhattan was once swampland. Pearl Street was named after the oysters that were there. The original inhabitants, the Lenape Indians, named the area "Manhatta," which means "Land of many hills." They resided in wigwams on the Upper East Side.

Back then, it would've been a national park on a par with Yellowstone or Yosemite. It was an estuary, where fresh water meets saltwater and biological diversity thrived. Manhattan was a lot colder four centuries ago. It is reported that the British walked bison across the ice from Staten Island. During Sandy's visit, in some ways, it reverted back to that state.

Here She Comes—The Perfect Storm

Sandy first hit the Caribbean, then the American coast. While it was a Category 2 hurricane off the coast of the Northeastern United States, the storm became the largest hurricane on record (as measured by diameter). Probes were shot into the eye to collect data. It made landfall in Brigantine, New Jersey, just north of Atlantic City, where waves were higher than 40 feet! That's great if you're a surfer, but not good if you're a nearby homeowner.

There was an unrelenting windstorm surge on top of high tides (the full moon created an astronomically high tide, which made it the worst possible time to hit). It was the perfect storm—meaning that all of the necessary attributes to create such a storm were present and in the right proportions.

New Jersey shore houses were demolished. Sandy then moved inland. There was a massive storm surge. The entire East Coast was impacted, and a total of 24 states were affected by the storm. West Virginia had three feet of snow. Sandy was 1,000 miles across. It was bigger than Katrina and Irene. There was 16 feet of water in some places. The National Weather Service said that waves up to 23 feet were reported as far away as southern Lake Huron in Michigan.

Seaside Heights, New Jersey, was completely decimated. Amusement rides that once crowned a pier there were dumped into the ocean.

Houses collapsed. Some turned upside down. Many wound up buried in the sand.

The City That Never Sleeps Closed Up Shop

Unfortunately, the Long Island Sound is built like a funnel. Water came pouring in. It is estimated that five hundred tons of water were dumped onto New York and New Jersey.

Air traffic in and out of New York and New Jersey was closed. In fact, more than 5,000 commercial flights scheduled for October 28 and 29 were canceled by the afternoon of the 28th. The New York Stock Exchange was shut down. The 108-year-old subway system stopped running. Amtrak canceled some services through October 29. Lower Manhattan had 14 feet of water.

ConEd pulled the plug on the electricity. So there was darkness. The Big Apple started running on flashlights, batteries, and candles. Brooklyn was submerged. Breezy Point, at the end of the Rockaway Peninsula in Queens, was in ruins. Over 100 houses burned to the ground there. Fires stretched New York's Emergency Services to the limit.

After the Deluge

Nine days after Sandy, there were freezing temperatures. The U.S. Army Corps of Engineers was called in to pump out millions of gallons of water.

New York City, New Jersey, and Long Island were like war zones. Over 8 million people (3,000,000 in Manhattan alone) were without power, some for weeks. It was a scene out of an end-of-the-world movie.

Few catastrophic events ever warrant the use of the active duty military and the reserves combined. To highlight the seriousness and the intensity of the situation, the National Guard activated the Emergency Management Assistance Company (EMAC), where partnered states may deploy their National Guard personnel to requesting states for humanitarian purposes under State Active Duty or under Title 32. The National Guard and the U.S. Air Force put as many as 45,000 troops in at least seven states on alert for possible duty. In Howard County, Maryland, workers tried to stop a sewage overflow caused by a power outage. Raw sewage spilled at a rate of 2,000,000 gallons per hour. It was unclear how much of it flowed into the Little Patuxent River.

Global Warming?

Some say, "This is a pattern of events that people are going to have to get used to." Others say we need a Green New Deal to combat climate change.

Was Sandy a once-in-a-100-years event? Or a sign of things to come? That's the trillion dollar question. We may not have too long to wait to find out the answer.

A warmer Arctic could've caused it. There is no doubt that the water in the ocean is warmer than it used to be. Therefore, decades from now, a storm like Sandy would be even more devastating—and perhaps much more lethal.

Takeaways

Sandy really was as bad as everybody said it would be. Once again, however, there still seemed to be people that didn't get it! They didn't evacuate. They weren't prepared. Many of them perished.

We must do better from this standpoint, but what does that really mean? We are privileged to live in these modern times when our National Weather Service produced very accurate predictions of Superstorm Sandy. The National Weather Service gave early predictions and further fine-tuned their forecast about Sandy's path over the ocean and landfall locations, wind speed, direction, and storm surges. They even predicted the changes in its behavior as it switched from a hurricane to a superstorm.

But what good is all the information if leaders are not ready to use it to make timely decisions? And, more importantly, what good are leaders if the people they lead do not listen to them? After all, it has been said that leadership is getting people to do what you want them to do, and I would add, without resorting to intimidation, humiliation, and fear.

The leaders received the information from the National Weather Service. In fact, we all received the same information and the leaders notified all of us; however, there were still people who were not prepared and did not evacuate, and the result was many deaths. What happened?

Leadership Happens

In all catastrophic events, people summon and muster the leadership traits and characteristics that lie within them to do extraordinary things to help their fellow human beings, and New Yorkers were no different.

At the direction of the adjutant general, the full-time staff members of the New York Army National Guard began its planning two weeks before the arrival of the storm. The reservist members were activated and brought on board one week before the storm. At H-96 hours, the New York military forces started the clock for the countdown to H hour when the storm would make landfall. As planners, we began our pre-combat inspections—or in this case our pre-SANDY LANDFALL inspections—of everything. Because of strong leadership and vision, an enormous amount of planning, budgeting, equipment preparation and pre-position (in addition to troop pre-position) needed to take place before H-hour, when the storm would make landfall.

The guidance from the adjutant general was to pre-position both troops as teams throughout the five boroughs of New York City and Long Island. This included maintenance personnel and teams, and critical equipment such as fuel, high-axle vehicles, chainsaws, rope and tackle, flashlights, batteries, and all appropriate personal protective equipment. All of the preparation proved to be needed. In the time approaching H-hour, the storm was raging as expected. The general framed his vision that the first thing he wanted New York City residents to see as they emerged from the safety of their homes, apartment buildings, and shelters after the storm passed was the presence of their military forces working and using their equipment, creating access for law enforcement and other first responders and conducting rescue missions. The extent of the damage started to become apparent at H+24 hours and beyond.

Three Leaders

Three leaders stand out in my mind as great examples of how ordinary people can summon the leadership characteristics and traits within themselves to do extraordinary things to help people, and they were on the ground when the storm hit. One such person was Battalion Chaplain Rabbi Raziel Amar. Three times, he requested to use my commander's HMMWV, along with the driver. Typically, if there were no other vehicles present, I let him use my vehicle or we traveled together to visit soldiers in different locations throughout the state. On one occasion, I found out to my surprise that the chaplain had been busy visiting the bodegas and stores along Lexington Avenue north of 125th Street, buying baby diapers. While he walked around the parks where the military was distributing food and water, praying and talking with New Yorkers, he found out that mothers needed diapers—and many stores in the impacted areas were either closed or destroyed—so they couldn't buy them. FEMA delivered more than sufficient food and water—but they did not deliver diapers.

On another occasion, the Rabbi saved the military public embarrassment. He noticed that the kosher meals that were loaded on trucks destined for the Hasidic communities were the wrong ones. And it would be considered a great insult to issue those meals to members of the Hasidic ultra-Orthodox Jewish community. So, we turned the trucks around, unloaded the meals, and continued the delivery and distribution with the correct meals. While this may seem a minor point, it is in fact a very important one. It would be the equivalent of delivering pork to a Muslim when he did not have anything to eat.

Another stand-out leader was Rich Wilson, a member of the board of directors of the Metropolitan Chapter of the USO. Rich showed up at the Harlem Armory office and asked the commander, "What do you need?" I quickly learned that when asked an open-ended question, you ask for the world. Rich ended up delivering two 20-person emergency shower trailers to the armory for the soldiers to take showers when they rotated to safety from the impacted areas. Additionally, he delivered boxes of snacks, energy drinks, juices, and sodas. He even delivered specialty trash bags that repelled rodents because there was no trash pickup and the trash was beginning to build up after several days. But that was not all.

Rich, along with President of the USO of Metropolitan New York, Brian Whiting, and Senior Vice President Jessica MacAndrews, were key in connecting us in the New York Army National Guard to trailers in North Carolina and other supply items used to set up morale welfare and recreation (MWR) tents. These tents were complete with flat screen television sets, video games, free vending machines, and hot beverages. North Carolina also sent volunteers to support up to 500 soldiers at a time. After the Thanksgiving holiday, when the cold winds began to blow across the old runways on Floyd Bennett Field in Brooklyn, we settled in for the long duration, continuing to deliver FEMA-provided meals and supplies to New Yorkers, using the parks as the assembly areas where people came to get water, food, and fuel.

Yet a third leader was JC Bravo, a captain who worked in my Operations Section. JC was always on the lookout for innovative ways to enhance the mission of the Guard by closely integrating the community with the local Guard unit. This is key to the success of the National Guard. I call it people helping people. And, to that end, JC introduced Rich to me through his network of contacts, and Rich leveraged the enormous resources of the USO. JC also coordinated having an Outback Steakhouse restaurant come to Floyd Bennett Field all the way from Philadelphia to serve the soldiers limitless meals of BBQ beef, chicken, salads, and warm beverages.

Again, as the temperature began to get cold after October, this was a kind gesture never to be forgotten by the soldiers and first responders at Floyd Bennett Field. They could return to the area after distributing meals, water, and fuel, and performing maintenance in 13- to 15-hour work shifts to rest and use the MWR tents, eat BBQ, and sleep. This went on 24 hours a day, seven days per week, in the rain, snow, and wind from October to the end of January, when the mission ended.

Our Share of the Task

We cannot stop natural disasters, but instead, only take measures to mitigate their impacts. Even though, when armed with knowledge, there are people who still do not get it. Good leaders need to react to take care of their people. Among the people there are always individuals ready to seize the opportunity to inspire others—by allowing the leader within to take charge in bad situations—and do extraordinary things.

All ordinary people can do extraordinary things when they allow the leader within to shine through. These leaders led with courage, love, integrity, and passion. And it showed.

***

CHAPTER 29

Cyber Warfare

People ask me all the time, "What keeps you up at night? And I say, 'Spicy Mexican food, weapons of mass destruction, and cyberattacks.'" —Dutch Ruppersberger

One area where we need to be on guard is cybersecurity. The urgency is so great because there is an immediate need for experts and warriors in the field and what we currently have is not enough.

Cyber has become an all-out war that is being waged quietly against the U.S. and its allies, both day and night. If the purpose of the U.S. military is to fight and win the nation's wars, and we typically win by going on the offensive in pursuit of our adversaries, then we need to remind ourselves that the cyber war that is ongoing is no different from any of the other wars that we have fought and won. Though we typically transition to a defensive posture to rest, refit, and refuel, we quickly do re-transition into the offensive.

In short, we win on the offense. But how do we transition into the offensive mode when most of our cyber warfare efforts have been limited to fighting in the defensive mode, reacting to mitigate the impacts from our adversary's offensive moves against us? In today's cyber engagement, we need to change from our defensive posture mindset to the offensive—or else I predict that we will be overrun in a few short years.

Ronald Reagan once said, "You cannot bargain from a position of weakness." Through his leadership we went on the offensive and pursued our adversary by building up massive military and weapons programs. We need to employ this same tactic in our approach to the cyber war.

The brilliant but uneducated strategist Nathan Bedford Forrest, a Confederate general in the American Civil War, was once asked which side would win a particular battle. His reply: "The one that gets there the fastest with the mostest." Well, we surely did not arrive at the line of departure for the cyber battle "fast," and we certainly did not bring much to fight with. Instead we continuously defend computer, command and control, intelligence, and surveillance systems, and react to China, Russia, Iran, and Korea's onslaught of our commercial and private assets.

Computer automation, cyberspace, and cloud-based concepts for information trafficking of personal, business, governmental, and even military intelligence are here now and are the trend of the future. Tomorrow is today, and the day after tomorrow is the focus of the cyber war.

Once Again, the First Step in Leadership is to Define Reality

Most cybersecurity employees are new to the arena. Any of them who are over 30 were not trained effectively and many of them don't even have degrees in the field. Some of them don't even have computer degrees!

In December of 2018, members of a Chinese espionage ring known as Advanced Persistent Threat Group 10 (aka APT 10, "Godkiller" and "Stone Panda") were charged with hacking NASA, the Jet Propulsion Laboratory, and IBM. As of this writing, the U.S. hasn't done much to respond. We don't seem to even have a policy regarding hacking.

I wrote a short essay back in 2013 about the significance of the cyberspace issue and safeguarding it. After spending 31 years in the service of our country in the army, I have developed a unique understanding and appreciation for preparedness and the importance of U.S. physical security. While we maintain and remain diligent about the physical security of our cities, bridges, tunnels, borders, and airports, we need to simultaneously prioritize and focus on another vulnerability that is becoming more apparent daily because it impacts the life of every American citizen now.

Securing cyberspace is the challenge that we face, and it is the common thread that is interwoven among all homeland security categories of borders, infrastructure, communications, law enforcement, and military. The degree of preparedness and the diligence and timeliness with which we can predict and mitigate the negative impacts of the threat will determine success both in our homeland and our allies' cybersecurity efforts.

Our law enforcement and national leaders in the U.S. and other western countries have always known that we needed to safeguard and protect cyberspace. During his first term of office, President Barack Obama identified cybersecurity as "one of the most serious economic and national security challenges we face as a nation, but one that we as a government or as a country are not adequately prepared to counter." This led to the President appointing a Cybersecurity Coordinator to synchronize the executive branch's efforts in May 2009. The Executive Branch Cybersecurity Coordinator began a campaign to immediately "promote cybersecurity awareness and digital literacy from our boardrooms to our classrooms..."

Additionally, he synchronized the recommendations from the Cyberspace Policy Review with the Comprehensive National Cybersecurity Initiative (CNCI), which was initiated under President George W. Bush as part of Homeland Security Presidential Directive 23 in January 2008. Of the 12 CNCI initiatives that range from Initiative #1 (managing the Federal Enterprise Network as a single network enterprise with Trusted Internet Connections, or TICs) to Initiative #12 (define the Federal role for extending cybersecurity into critical infrastructure domains), Initiative #8 (expand cyber education) was the key focus of the Executive Branch Cybersecurity Coordinator. The coordinator supported a CNCI recommendation that it will take a "national strategy, similar to the effort to upgrade science and mathematics education in the 1950s, in order to meet the challenge" regarding the shortage of trained cybersecurity personnel.

In continuing with his cybersecurity agenda, President Obama elevated the issue of cybersecurity as a national security issue. During his second term in office, he signed the cybersecurity executive order on February 12, 2013. As stated in the Policy, this was the result of "repeated cyber intrusions into critical infrastructure demonstrating the need for improved cybersecurity..." The policy statement goes on to state that cyber threats to critical infrastructure continue to grow and represent one of the most "serious national security challenges" we must confront, and it highlights that "the policy of the United States is to enhance the security and resilience of the nation's critical infrastructure and to maintain a cyber environment that encourages efficiency, innovation, and economic prosperity..."

This was a game changer because it took the issue of cybersecurity and its significance to mainstream America from the highest levels of government. The realization that nations, terrorists, and 'hacktivists' groups use the web as their weapon of choice to conduct "cyber-intrusions" and distribute denial-of-service (DDoS) made the President, business leaders, military leaders, and ordinary citizens pay close attention to this issue. But most efforts across the whole spectrum of cybersecurity are defensive in nature.

In order to beat the attackers, we need to go on the offensive in pursuit of the cyber intruders. Cyberspace has been around, but information trafficking of personal, government, military, and business information in that space—along with cloud-based concepts—is new and less than 15 years old. And the advent of our adversaries and criminal elements disrupting that space for illegal gains and just plain mischief has created the need for cybersecurity. The problem is so big and widespread that it is now a matter of national security. The need for cybersecurity will continue to grow and the demand will be high.

Self Defense

Jim Malone, played by Sean Connery in the 1987 movie *The Untouchables,* said something akin to, "Don't show up to a gun battle with a knife." The expression has been emulated in more than 20 movies since 2000, so it has obviously resonated with the American psyche.

Some people see a correlation between deterrence in cyber and nuclear warfare. John Yoo, a Berkeley law professor, says, "Offensive nuclear weapons are relatively cheap. It is defensive systems that are very expensive."

It has been reported that each mission to drop one nuclear bomb would cost the U.S. about a quarter billion dollars. After all, intercontinental ballistic missiles, bombers, and subs aren't cheap. But we have spent trillions on our defense and deterrent system.

Spending on the part of government, as well as private organizations, has increased on encryption, firewalls, malware, spyware, and virus protectors, as well as intrusion detectors. It's a computer cyberspace race on the order and magnitude of the nuclear arms race. While we are familiar with and prepared to deal with the latter, we are still struggling to deal with the former and we continue to be very vulnerable.

Relevant Background

After the Chinese stole plans for the F-35 stealth fighter from Lockheed and North Korea hacked Sony, General Paul Nakasone took over U.S. Cyber Command. Army Cyber Command is part of CYBERCOM. Nakasone had experience in cyber operations and signal intelligence, which is intelligence derived from electronic systems used by foreign targets, such as computers, radar, and weapons systems. The National Security Administration's (NSA) main mission is limited to gathering information about foreign terrorists, individuals, and organizations. Nakasone's NSA assignment came with a promotion to four-star general.

The U.S. Cyber Command (CYBERCOM) is intended to be a Functional Combatant Command similar to the other nine current Combatant Commands: U.S. Africa Command (AFRICOM): U.S. Northern Command (NORTHCOM), U.S. Southern Command (SOUTHCOM), U.S. European Command (EUCOM), U.S. Pacific Command (PACOM), U.S. Central Command (CENTCOM), U.S. Special Operations Command (SOCOM), U.S. Strategic Command (STRATCOM), and U.S. Transportation Command (TRANSCOM). With this status comes resources and a direct communications link to the President of the United States.

Specifically, CYBERCOM is the fourth functional combatant command, which is different from the geographic combatant commands. Placing the battle against cyberattacks in the organizational structure among the other notable organizations is a great start, but we need more. The agency has to be better equipped to confront the digital threats of the 21st century. Cyber hacking is an epidemic, of sorts.

China's goal is to replace the U.S. as the world's superpower, and cyber warfare is the main thread that is interwoven throughout all of the elements that define the term "superpower." Elements such as currency, military, economic, homeland security, allied security, communications, intelligence, and surveillance all need access to a safe, secure cyberspace to function properly. Cyber superiority has become equal to air superiority. You cannot have one without the other. We need to catch up fast and surpass our adversaries.

Fort Knox Doesn't Exist Anymore

Through its Advanced Persistent Threat 10 espionage ring, China tapped into the Department of Energy, NASA, and the U.S. Navy. China was also able to compromise data from companies in a dozen other countries, from Brazil to the United Arab Emirates. In its threat to steal intellectual property, they have targeted not only individual companies, but, more specifically, managed service providers (MSPs). MSPs are the businesses that provide IT infrastructure like data storage or password management.

China's hackers are not only sophisticated—they're relentless. More than 90 percent of the Justice Department's cases alleging economic espionage over the past seven years involve China. This will continue to be an area of tension between the United States and "The Sleeping Giant."

On the surface, the way the Chinese go about their hacking seems very legitimate. Only it's not. Microsoft Word attachments can be malicious spear phishing attempts, loaded with customized remote access Trojans. These viruses let hackers gain access to and control the computer much like a skimmer on an ATM machines. It can steal usernames and passwords.

China and the United States came to an agreement in 2015 that they won't hack each other's private sector interests. APT10 started before the agreement was put in place. However, there is no indication that China has stopped its cyber hacking espionage activities, despite the agreement.

Check This Site

Security expert Troy Hunt created a website in December 2013 to help people determine if their email and password has been shared. The URL is www.HaveIBeenPwned.com (with "pwned" pronounced like "poned"). The initiative started after Adobe was hacked in 201_, where 153 million addresses were shared. At the time, there were only five known security breaches: Stratfor, Gawker, Adobe, Yahoo Voices, and Sony. These days, it seems as if there is one a week. In November of 2018, Marriott announced that five million unencrypted passport numbers were snatched from its system. Subsequently, they were hacked at least twice more and have confessed that hackers gained access to over 300 million hotel guests' personal information, including credit card numbers.

One of the reasons why the Chinese are narrowing the gap with the U.S. militarily is their theft of designs and other sensitive data. There is supposedly a truce in effect, but the Chinese seem to be good at camouflaging it. Beijing is up to its old tricks and knows how to hide it.

There's also an uncanny resemblance between Chinese and American military weaponry. Advanced missiles, drone technology—even stealth aircraft—all seem very Western in their design and function. For example, the Chinese J-20 is very similar to the U.S.'s F-22 fighter jet. Their stealth fighter FC-31 Gyrfalcon is seen as a knockoff of Lockheed's F-35.

China is very good at getting into U.S. defense contractor's computer systems through various types of cyber warfare. An enormous amount of time, talent, and money is invested to research and develop systems; to have another country steal the products and replicate them in less than half the time and money it took to develop them is frustrating (to say the least).

Be Aware of the Danger, but Recognize the Opportunity

Between September 2017 and August 2018, U.S. employers posted nearly 314,000 jobs for cybersecurity positions. According to the National Initiative for Cybersecurity Education, if these jobs could be filled, it would boost the country's current cyber workforce of 714,000 by 40 percent. Unfortunately, only recently has formal training existed, and it has been relatively inadequate.

Companies and government entities are looking for people with computer science, programming, or computer engineering backgrounds, and are open to those with backgrounds in statistics and math.

ifications and experience in intrusion detection.
er boot camps and community college programs that
ortage. Yet, there is a gap of nearly 3 million cyber
all, this matter wasn't exactly mentioned in either of
gatrends* or *Future Shock,* or in any of Faith Popcorn's
books. modern-day concern.

Companies are relying on artificial intelligence (AI) and machine learning, but this often does little more than mitigate the challenge. Many smaller companies are attacked—as a way to get to their larger brethren—and they can't keep up. This serious problem is rampant.

Many computer science curricula in colleges, surprisingly, don't mandate taking courses in cybersecurity. Established boot camps that educate and help people land jobs include Securest Academy in Denver, Open Cloud Academy in San Antonio, and Evolve Security in Chicago.

There are also over a dozen two-year college cybersecurity programs spread across the country. A hybrid between a boot camp and community college program is the City College of Chicago (CCC), which partners with the Department of Defense on a free cybersecurity training program for active military service members.

All of the previously mentioned efforts thus far are reactive and defensive in nature. Leadership needs to elevate the priority and switch the focus from being on the defense to going on the offense. This will be a good start to effectively dealing with the threat. Offense involves three elements: deny and disrupt; incentivize and budget massive amounts of funding to create opportunities for cyber creativity; and cyber innovation.

The crux of the matter is this is just one more area where we need to remain on guard.

***

EPILOGUE

Going Forward

"Not everything that is faced can be changed, but nothing can be changed until it is faced." – James Baldwin

As human beings, we will always have human issues. In this century alone, Americans have endured terrorist attacks, lethal hurricanes, superstorms, cyber warfare, and a multitude of other challenges, both natural and man-made. While they're happening, they seem insurmountable. But time heals the wounds and we move on. Until the next crisis comes along.

I mentioned earlier in this book that the next Ebola was going to happen. I suggested that it could be a fire, a flood, a famine, or a pandemic. Well, as I bring this book to a close, we are in the crosshairs of COVID-19, the disease caused by a new strain of the coronavirus. As I understand it, coronavirus has several strains that cause different diseases.

It has been said that we haven't been under warfare as intense as this since World War II.

Pandemic = Universal

As of this writing, and although these numbers are controversial, the outbreak has infected more than 35,000,000 people in over 185 countries and territories and is continuing to spread. All of Africa's 54 countries have confirmed cases. The prospect of a mass outbreak is particularly alarming for that continent, which has a shortage of about 1.8 million health workers (that is already suffering the world's largest disease burden), according to the World Health Organization (WHO). The UN states that, in 2018, nearly half a million people in sub-Saharan Africa died from AIDS-related causes alone.

Daily life in the United States has become more and more disrupted as the virus spreads. This includes entertainment venues, sports, churches, eating establishments, and other businesses. The stock market has taken a beating the likes of which haven't been seen since the days of the Great Depression nearly a century ago. The government is on track to test federal budget records hit after the 2008 financial crisis, when annual red ink soared past $1.5 trillion.

School closings have affected millions of children. The shutting of so many schools across the United States inflicts massive economic, academic, and social repercussions. It forces millions of parents to stay home from work to look after their children, handcuffing businesses and local economies. Needless to say, this disease is devastating.

On top of that, there's no denying that the U.S. is presently in the midst of huge crises and turmoil and is, as a nation, very deeply divided. There is not only the coronavirus, but there are also nationwide protests as a result of the killing of George Floyd, a black man killed by a white police officer. Even the status of the military is in question, with military leaders breaking with the president on how the military, including the National Guard, should be used—something we've never seen before.

Optimist and Pessimist

Windows of opportunity open and close. That's why it is essential that we be on guard each and every day so that we can mitigate disaster or minimize the carnage. We must soldier on as Captain Dan McNally did during 9.11. We must act caringly and astutely as ordinary citizens doing extraordinary things, as Rabbi Raziel Amar, Rich Wilson, and JC Bravo did during Superstorm Sandy. We must prepare our offspring to tackle cyber and biological warfare. And it behooves us, much like General Honoré did during Hurricane Katrina, to know an opponent's likes and dislikes so we can anticipate their vulnerabilities. Toward that end we can often force our enemies to react in a certain way.

Like no other time ever, leaders need to put systems in place to get the right things done. Time is of the essence. Leadership is about getting people to do what you want (and need) them to do in a swift timeframe without resorting to humiliation, intimidation, or fear. It has been proven time and time again that those three approaches are not healthy and just don't work.

Leaders have to be able to take charge and assure the people that they will be safe and that they are the one individual who is looking out for their welfare, and will lead them through whatever comes their way, much like Churchill led the British people during WWII. And they have to be able to communicate that trust in no uncertain terms.

The Guard Gets Mobilized

The reality is that the book still needs to be written about COVID-19. It is such a complex situation with no end currently in sight. There will surely be lessons drawn from this global pandemic.

As this book goes to press, National Guard members are on the front lines of the spreading coronavirus. Operating under the direction of their respective state governors, the members' mission (as of now) includes disinfecting public spaces, distributing food, assisting with transportation and logistical support of health officials, and collecting and delivering samples. They are also dealing with protestors, both violent and peaceful.

The National Guards of the 50 states, three territories and the District of Columbia have a very deep bench of almost 450,000 experienced and proven Air and Army National Guard professionals. They have unique capabilities such as Civil Support Teams and CERFPs (CBRNE Enhanced Response Force Package) that could provide local first responders with additional resources.

Things Aren't Always What They Seem

To a large extent, the perception is greater than the reality. And it is imperative that the leader not be insensitive to the concerns of the people. It is crucial that the leader, "Do something!" As they say at the Academy, "We'll discuss the merits of what you did later."

First and foremost, it is important to recognize that leaders are not always going to be right. But, if they make good decisions **most of the time**—or when it is necessary—then they'll be treated as heroes, replete with proverbial accolades and parades. However, if you as a leader are invariably making bad decisions, the saying goes, "We'll skin you alive and shoot you!"

I cannot stress enough how indispensable it is in this day and age as a leader to make good decisions. And, in order to make good decisions, it is fundamental that you have the right tools. I submit to you that the main tools necessary are what I call the four pillars of leadership: courage, love, integrity, and passion. These are vital and are what good knowledge management is about. Put them in your leadership toolkit and you will be the leader you always envisioned you would be. Most importantly, the world will thank you for it.

Only in the Darkness Can You See the Stars

I believe that America will come together to defeat the coronavirus and resolve the differences that divide us. When America has needed leaders in the past, leaders, national or local, have stepped forward.

The following thought resonates with me from my friend Manuel Ron. Assistant Professor and Assistant Dean for the Graduate Business School at Mercy College, Professor Ron eloquently stated, "People can choose many ways to live their lives and conduct their business. And this choice is purely personal and changeable. But when you pick up the mantle of leadership in life or business, whether you intend to pick it or whether you pick it up by the fact, not aware of your implicit role, you are picking up the *duty* to 'do the right thing.' And, unlike *responsibility* which you can chose to accept or not, *duty* is infused in leadership, giving you no choices except to 'do the right thing.' And, in doing the 'right thing,' you may at times find that you are last. Your family, either defined legally or by the fact of your ties, comes before you. Your employees and shareholders come before you. And whatever remains, if anything, is for you, and for you to share. So, if the notion of *duty* is too much for you, or you believe *duty* is a choice, or you believe that 'the right thing' is fundamentally subjective, then, please don't ask to lead me and I will not ask to lead you—because it won't work out. But if we find ourselves in each other's orbit, you know what you can expect from me and what I will expect from you."

The whole purpose of being "on guard" is so the people who you, as a leader, serve, can "Keep Calm and Carry On." Or, as the Italian posters in the windows during the coronavirus outbreak read, "Andrà' tutto bene" (Everything's gonna be all right).

POSTSCRIPT

If I have inspired just one person to follow a passion that they have identified as a result of reading this book, then I will look at my life as having left a legacy to future generations. I'm not going to say I can find it for you because that's on you. But, hopefully, a lightbulb has (or will) come on.

You identify this passion and have made a decision or have already acted on it, knowing that it is unique to you. It is something that you have within you and doesn't cost you anything. You don't need to go buy it at Walmart. You come hardwired with it. It's a matter of awareness of first being awakened to it, and then you go kick it off. Having identified and reconciled a number of things, you may be at a point where, "It doesn't matter anymore," to use the words and imbue the courage and integrity of Dr. King.

I think when you get to that point, you transform. You become unstoppable in your quest and in your passion for this thing. You start to think about it differently and now there's a cause. A purpose. If that can happen to just one person, this book will have been an extremely worthwhile endeavor.

ACKNOWLEDGMENTS

As you have surmised by now, I have great respect for the United States military. As delineated, there are six military officers in particular that I was privileged to work with in my 30+ years of service that deserve special recognition: Captain Dan McNally, Colonel Carl Pfeiffer, Colonel Mark Moser, Colonel Dave Cox, Colonel Stephanie Dawson, and General Timothy McKeithen. I have mentioned their influence on me in this book. There were many other people that were extremely influential in my life, but these six military officers stand head and shoulders above the rest.

I was also privileged to work with many Non-Commissioned Officers (NCOs), including Command Sergeant Major Joe Boledovic. Collectively, one cannot find a more seasoned group of dedicated and committed professionals who do not get the full credit they deserve—and they would prefer it remain that way. It is not a coincidence that one hundred percent of soldiers who attended a basic training course would have only positive things to say about, and have fond memories of and profound respect for ninety-nine percent of their sergeants. When soldiers successfully complete basic training and report to their units, it is the sergeants who they report to. And it is the sergeants who have the responsibility for their individual training and professional growth, while the officer is accountable for their collective training.

As an officer who was privileged to serve as an enlisted service member before transitioning to the Officer Corps, I am among the few who experienced both NCO leadership and officer leadership styles firsthand, and believe me when I tell you they are very different. I found the majority of the NCO's leadership styles to be genuine and unbiased toward their soldiers and focused on the Army's mission to fight and win America's wars. However, this book is about the officers who I spent 20-plus years with—from when I was a newly commissioned second lieutenant up until my retirement as a lieutenant colonel. When I finished serving my time in the military, my adjutant general had a "retire, I don't owe you anything" leadership style.

My father, Bishop Francis Eustace Harris, passed away two months prior to my retirement from active duty in the Army National Guard, so I underwent a lot of change at that time. I did some soul searching. When I think back on his and my life, he was the leader who inspired me the most. My father left Sierra Leone at age 19 for London. In his late 40s he obtained his doctorate in divinity and shortly after that followed with his doctorate in metaphysics.

I'd also like to thank my mother, Elvira, my sisters, Safee and Frances, and my children, Daniel Jr. and Antonia-Isis. My younger brother, Dr. Peter Edward Francis Harris II, whom I admired tremendously and had a lot of respect for, also passed during the writing of this book. In many ways, Peter was my leadership anchor because at an early age he would often refer to me as the "leader of the pack." Subconsciously, I embodied the role and at an early age this began to shape my attitude toward my siblings, including a focus on developing solutions and forward thinking. Because whenever he got into trouble with the other boys at school and in the neighborhood, he would tell them, "I'm going to get my big brother and when he comes here, he will straighten you all out."

Thanks to those who read first drafts of the book and provided valuable feedback and support in areas such as fact-checking and readability, including First Sergeant Lloyd Headley, Ana Petrovich, Rich Wilson, Vicky and Ed Theis, Delroy Walters, Andrae Evans, Rick Saldan and Roy Diehl.

Thank you as well to editors Christopher G. Murray and Andrea Quarracino.

GLOSSARY

AAR – After Action Review
AIT – Advanced Individual Training
ANOC – Advanced Non-Commissioned Officers Course
AO – Administrative Officer
AOIC – Assistant Officer in Charge
ARNG – Army National Guard
BCT – Brigade Combat Team
BLC – Basic Leaders Course (formerly BNOC)
BNOC – Basic Non-Commissioned Officers Course
CBRNE – Chemical, Biological, Radiological, Nuclear and Explosive
CENTCOM – United States Central Command
CLRT-X – Command Logistics Review Team
CSM – Command Sergeant Major
CONUS – Contiguous United States
DASB – Division Aviation Support Battalion
DHS – Department of Homeland Security
FEMA – Federal Emergency Management Association
FOB – Forward Operating Base
FSB – Forward Support Battalion (no longer used)
HSC – Headquarters and Supply Company
HaDR – Humanitarian Assistance Disaster Relief
HTAR – How The Army Runs
IA – Iraqi Army
IBSF – Iraqi Border Security Forces
IP – Iraqi Police
ISF – Iraqi Security Forces
JACO – Joint Action Control Office
JDAM – Joint Direct Attack Mission
LTC – Lieutenant Colonel
NCO – Non-commissioned Officer
NGB – National Guard Bureau
OCS – Officer Candidate School
OCONUS – Outside Continental United States
QRF – Quick Reaction Force
RDAC – Recruiting District Assistance Council
RPG – Rocket Propelled Grenade
SLC – Senior Leaders Course (formerly ANOC)
SAMS – School of Advanced Military Studies
UN—United Nations
WHO – World Health Organization

About the Authors

Lieutenant Colonel (Ret.) Daniel E. Harris is a 30-year veteran of the U.S. armed forces and lives in Tobyhanna in the Pocono Mountains of Northeast Pennsylvania. He is the founder and CEO of Muddy Boots Leadership, LLC. Muddy Boots is a leadership development organization that specializes in developing managers and supervisors into leaders. LTC Harris is also an adjunct professor teaching graduate-level business courses for the Masters of Science degree in Organizational Leadership at Mercy College.

He has led diverse organizations and teams to accomplish organizational goals. He has leadership development expertise in talent management with a focus on identifying and nurturing leadership potential, giving managers the leadership foundation to transition to executive-level roles. He has strategic level experience from working at the DoD and can leverage experiential learning solutions through teaching, coaching and mentoring leaders to perform at their best and achieve lasting impact on people and organizations.

LTC (Ret.) Harris has developed learning solutions based on learning theory and was responsible for implementing and delivering leadership development and performance management strategies, as well as onboarding officers and NCOs, in multiple army organizations. He has directed and was responsible for the leadership programs for his staff as well as service members from both foreign and U.S. military, with responsibility to measure the learning, the impact of the program and leadership strategy.

Harris is a proven leader with the ability to identify, develop, and leverage junior leaders' strengths and cross-level competencies to capitalize on individual experiences and motivate teams, as well as to focus and execute the strategic vision to achieve his unit organizational goals in both the Continental United States (CONUS) and Outside Continental United States (OCONUS).

FJ Felsburg is a writer based in Western North Carolina. He spent decades in leadership roles in both for-profit and non-profit organizations, having primarily worked in publishing and global marketing. He can be reached at www.SpokenAndWrittenWords.com, @fjfelsburg, or frankfelsburg@gmail.com.

Made in United States
Orlando, FL
15 January 2023